# Art of Poetry, Volume 15

## Pre-C20th poems for KS3 pupils

With special thanks to my colleagues at the wonderful @Team_English1 for their help, support and suggestions for poems, and to my family for letting me hide away and keep writing.

Published by Peripeteia Press Ltd.

First published September 2017

ISBN: 978-1-9997376-1-0

Peripeteia.webs.com

# Contents

# Introduction

Finding these poems has been both fun and frustrating. Ideally, for instance, I would have liked to include truly wonderful children's poems, such as T. S. Eliot's *Macavity the Mystery Cat* and A. A. Milne's *The King's Breakfast*. To do so I would have had to bend the Pre-C20th assignation to include poems written by poets born before the twentieth century. As you can see from the contents page I was prepared to be this flexible if I felt the poem justified it. It was, however, the demands of copyright that prevented the inclusion of those two poems, with the latter policed by the Disney corporation. As far as possible I have checked that the remaining poems are free to use. If you are aware that I have infringed any copyright please accept my apologies and get in touch.

Ideally I would also have a better balance of male and female voices in the anthology. The fact that it is so dominated by men reflects historical gender imbalances in education and in literature. I didn't include token poems by female writers to even up the balance because each poem here has been selected for its potential in teaching poetry. If discussions of gender and representation are one off-shoot of this, that would be a bonus, but is not the main objective. Similarly there is a lack of voices from across the classes and from non-white English speakers. Though William Barnes and Robert Burns do employ non-standard English the anthology is dominated by variations of the standard version. Again, this reflects the dominant forces historically controlling and shaping literature. If colleagues can point to poems and poets whose voices I could, or perhaps should, have included I'd be delighted to produce a second, expanded edition of the anthology in the near future.

The fun part has been reading lots and lots of terrific poems, researching the poets, coming up with the teaching ideas and actually writing this material. To be honest, when the idea of producing an anthology of pre-C20th poems for KS3 pupils was first suggested to me I was somewhat sceptical about whether it could be done well. My instinct and practice has been to use more modern poetry with this age group. And there are lots of great modern poems that engage the minds, hearts and imaginations of KS3 pupils. Much harder, I thought, to find older, more canonical poems that would provide the right balance of challenge and accessibility. Researching this book proved my instincts wrong. Ideally, pupils would have a mixed diet of poetry and of literature more broadly, something new, something old, something borrowed. And, as many colleagues, have commented, it is always surprising and heartening to see how well young pupils can cope with really quite complex literary material. If we underestimate children's capacities we will not be ambitious enough in the material we offer them.

Almost as important as the exposure to great work is the way in which this work is presented. The literary diet needs to be varied, but so too does the ways in which poetry is approached. Endless analysis or spotting of typical poetic features in preparation for GCSE will kill pupils' enjoyment of poems and impose severe limits on the way they respond. Far better if analytical, brain-based responses are leavened with more creative and performance based engagement. Hence the suggested teaching activities that accompany each poem in the anthology offer a range of approaches. Sometimes the focus will be on the poet's technique and on developing pupils' appreciation of a writer's craft. Sometimes the poems will be vehicles for introducing, developing of consolidating literary knowledge, such as the technical vocabulary of poetry - metaphor, stanza, metre and so forth. Other ideas, however, promote creative writing in both prose and poetic form. Developing writing is worthwhile on its own terms, but better writers also become better readers, and vice versa.

However, it's no good, I believe, giving pupils a vague title, such as Winter, and asking them to write a poem on this theme. A few might be able to produce something, but the work is likely to tend to cliché and be either shapeless or contorted by rhyme. Most pupils, I expect, will struggle as I did when given similarly unstructured tasks when I was a pupil. This sort of exercise is analogous to sitting an untutored child in front of a piano and asking them to compose a tune.

Instead we need to build pupils' ability to write in poetic form, small steps at a time. For example, cloze exercises encourage pupils to step into the writer's shoes and make the sorts of decisions a writer makes. As we all know, in poetry, each word matters, so thinking hard about why one word rather than another similar word should be used is fundamental. From single words, pupils can be encouraged to fill in bigger gaps, such as guessing a withheld title or completing lines that the teacher has blanked out of the poem. Poets learn to write through imitation of poems they admire. The poems in this anthology also provide models for longer written responses. The model may be formal, such as the sonnet or the epigram, or in terms of subject matter, such as the personification of vices in Spenser's **The Fairie Queene**. The written response may be a parody, exaggerating the poet's style or a pastiche, imitating it. Whichever teaching ideas you take up, the challenge is to get pupils to write about and in response to poetry in a variety of forms. Yes, teach them how to write an analytical paragraph and even a whole literary critical essay, but also engage their imaginations, fire their creativity.

Another creative way for pupils to engage with poetry is, of course, through performance. The fantastic **Poetry by Heart** project has had a hugely positive impact, loosening the tight relationship between poetry and high stakes assessment and helping pupils to connect with poetry in more profound and personal ways. Hearing a poem spoken from heart is also a much more powerful experience for an audience than hearing it read out. Check the Poetry by Heart website for many great examples. Lots of the poems in this anthology lend themselves to being learned by heart, not least because many of them are quite short. Why not carry a bit of Sappho's poetry around with you or some of **Paradise Lost**? At the very least it might help to pass the time while waiting for public transport.

Group performances of poetry can also be exciting and develop appreciation. Give different poems to pupils working in groups, ask them to read their poem through a couple of times and then come up with a way of reading it that will really express the poem. Initially pupils may opt for conservative and obvious approaches, such as each member of a group reading a line in turn. But, given time, given advice, given encouragement many pupils will be prepared to move into more dynamic readings. Ask the group to decide when and how to use choric voices, how they can vary the volume, the pacing and the tone of their delivery. Encourage them to think about the performance of the poem as being like the performance of a piece of music. When is the climax, the crescendo, which bits could be quiet or slow or menacing or gentle? If you or they are keen on drama, you could also consider the visual presentation by the group. They don't have to simply line up and read, they could choregraph their performance adding movement and action to suit the poem. If the experience of poetry is fun as well as challenging, it will be rewarding too.

You will have noticed, no doubt, that the poems have been arranged not by year group or thematically, but chronologically. I considered the former arrangement, but decided it would impose artificial constraints. You will be the best person to judge whether your Year 7 class will cope with a complex poem or whether it might better suit a Year 9. And, of course, it depends what you're going to do with the poem. Each poem is accompanied by some brief biographical notes, a little bit of pract. crit. style analysis and some teaching ideas. My only advice is to keep back the formal, critical essay until at least Year 9. In my opinion, too much analytical work, too soon can smother pupils' creative engagement and enjoyment of literature. Arranging the poems in this chronological order also helps chart the protean nature of poetry and takes us on a journey through many centuries and cultures., styles and forms. I hope you and your pupils will enjoy the journey.

Tread softly, because you tread on my dreams

W. B. YEATS

# Sappho [630 BC - 580 BC]

## *Love*

And love shook my senses -
A wind across mountains
Randomly lashing the trees.

## The Poet

Little is known for certain about the life of the Greek poet, Sappho. We do know that she lived on the island of Lesbos and that she wrote many poems, perhaps as much as 10,000. From these poems only around 650 lines have survived and these are mostly in fragmentary form. One of the first poets to write lyric poetry, i.e. poetry in the first person, intimate 'I' voice, Sappho's major themes were love and the lives of women. Over the ages, the frankness of her descriptions of love has been both celebrated and censored, with Pope Gregory VII [1020 -1085] going as far as to order all her poetry to be burnt. A feminist icon, Sappho's thematic and stylistic influence on literature has been profound and widespread.

## The Poem

Often in her poetry, Sappho presents love as a bittersweet experience. The first line of this poem, or fragment from a longer poem, is ambiguous: Is having your senses shaken a good or bad thing? If we've been shaken by an experience, commonly this means it has troubled us in some profound way. On the other hand, shaking our senses suggests that love can change the way we perceive the world and open fresh perspectives. Sometimes we need to be shaken.

The poem, or fragment, opens *in media res*, in the middle of action. Something has already happened, as if off stage, something that was linked to the poem's opening word, the conjunction 'and'. Sappho immediately provides an arresting concrete image to make the emotional experience tangible; to experience love is like being lashed by a mountain wind. Clearly, the wind is a mysterious, ungovernable and unpredictable force, while the mountains create a sense of epic scale. The idea of the unpredictability of love is reinforced by the adverb 'randomly' and the speaker's ambivalence about experiencing love is further emphasised by the violently onomatopoeic verb, 'lashed', with its suggestion of whips and pain. In contrast to the dynamic, external force of the wind, the speaker presents themselves in static images, as a mountain and as trees.

Stylistically the poem is lean, intense, economical with its words. A major emotion is swiftly introduced and an image follows which helps us to imagine experiencing it. Sappho's poem exemplifies the poetic dictum that poems should use the fewest words to create the most powerful effect. The tight style of her poetry and her use of metaphor had a profound influence on the Imagist poets, in particular, as we will see later in the poem by Hilda Doolittle whose shortening of her name to just H.D. itself is indicative of the principle of concentration and intensification. Another example of Sappho's influence is fellow Imagist, Ezra Pound's, poem, 'the days are not full enough/ the nights are not full enough/ and life slips by/ like a field mouse not shaking the grass'.

## The Teaching Ideas

The major ideas to communicate through this poem are that poems are often concentrated, intense forms of language, like shots of expresso coffee; that poets try to describe familiar or universal experiences in ways that make us think differently about them and that metaphor is a key poetic device for achieving this modification of perception. The following activities encourage both analytical and creative engagement with Sappho's poem.

➜   Highlight the importance each image contributes to the poem and the power of metaphor by giving small groups of pupils different clozed version of the poem, with the task to fill in the blanked-out words. [Give them a couple of minutes only.]

### Group 1:
And _____ shook my senses
A wind across mountains
Randomly _____ the trees.

### Group 2:
And love shook my senses
A _____ across mountains
_____ lashing the trees.

### Group 3:
And love _____ my senses
A wind across _____

Randomly lashing the trees.

➔    Gather responses and discuss options as way of focusing attention on the poet's choices of words.

➔    Creative work: Individually pupils pick another emotion - hate, envy, pity, kindness, sadness should all work well - and write a three-line poem following Sappho's example. Sharing these poems with their peers, pupils could read out just the last two lines with the rest of the class tasked with guessing the emotion from the metaphor. A whole class 'emotion' poem can then be arranged by the teacher.

Ovid [43 BC - ?]

## Extract from Metamorphoses, translated by Sir Samuel Garth, John Dryden, et al

### The Story of Medusa's Head

The heroe with his just request complies,
Shows, how a vale beneath cold Atlas lies,
Where, with aspiring mountains fenc'd around,
He the two daughters of old Phorcus found.
Fate had one common eye to both assign'd,
Each saw by turns, and each by turns was blind.
But while one strove to lend her sister sight,
He stretch'd his hand, and stole their mutual light,
And left both eyeless, both involv'd in night.

Thro' devious wilds, and trackless woods he past,
And at the Gorgon-seats arriv'd at last:
But as he journey'd, pensive he survey'd,
What wasteful havock dire Medusa made.
Here, stood still breathing statues, men before;
There, rampant lions seem'd in stone to roar.
Nor did he, yet affrighted, quit the field,
But in the mirror of his polish'd shield
Reflected saw Medusa slumbers take,
And not one serpent by good chance awake.
Then backward an unerring blow he sped,
And from her body lop'd at once her head.
The gore prolifick prov'd; with sudden force
Sprung Pegasus, and wing'd his airy course.

## The Poet

A Roman poet who enjoyed immense success and popularity in his life time and who was married three times, Ovid ended his life exiled by the emperor Augustus. Ovid's most famous work is Metamorphoses, a hugely influential work which contains over 250 myths.

## The Poem

Like his fellow heroes from Greek mythology, Perseus has been given a seemingly impossible, probably fatal task; to bring back the head of the gorgon, Medusa. The gorgon, Medusa, her of the quaint live-snakes hair-do and eyes that quite literally petrify anyone who looks at her. Having collected some useful help, equipment and advice, not least the winged horse, Pegasus, Perseus arrives at the wild place where the gorgons live and finds a cunning way to kill the monster. Sometimes this wild place is described as a barren island at the end of the world, in other versions, such as this one from the seventeenth century it is reached through wild woods.

This elegant, swift-moving version is written in heroic couplets; rhymed lines of iambic pentameter. The writers move through the action quickly and leave little time to build mood and atmosphere.

## The Teaching Ideas

➔ Pupils could write their own version of this episode in Perseus' story. Writing in prose, they should concentrate on building up tension through generating an atmosphere of dread. Changing the narrative point of view to Perseus' will help, as would concentration on describing the setting in creepy detail. Alternatively, they could join another Greek hero, Theseus, as he descends into the heart of the King Minos' labyrinth to face the minotaur. In either case, emphasise that you want pupils to spend as much time as possible on the build-up to the action, rather than the action itself, although they are, of course, allowed to write this in as much vivid, bloody detail as they, or you, can stomach.

➜ Hopefully your pupils will be keen to read the whole of Perseus' story now and there are plenty of versions available online and in book form. If they already know this one, they could research other Greek myths.

➜ Collect your pupils' knowledge of characters from Greek myths. Which heroes do they know? Theseus, Jason, Hercules, Odysseus? What about the Greek Gods, Zeus, Athene, Hades, Aphrodite and the rest of their crew? Or other characters, such as the singer, Orpheus, the inventor Daedalus, the greedy and foolish King Midas, the blind seer Tiresias or gloomy Charon the ferryman? What about the villains and monsters? Hades, Medea, King Minos; the hydra, the cyclops, the sirens, harpies and, of course, the three-headed dog, Cerberus who we are about to meet in the next extract, from **The Divine Comedy**. These are all seminal characters who helped shape western literatures conceptions of heroes, villains, monsters and gods. Consider, for example, what the heroes might have in common and how they relate to their modern offspring, superheroes. Such characters crop up time and again in literature in various forms. A fun and useful way to get to know them is to produce top trump cards with ratings for strength, courage, danger, cunning etc.

# Dante Alighieri [1265 -1321]

## *Extract from The Divine Comedy, translated by Henry Cary*

In the third circle I arrive, of showers
Ceaseless, accursed, heavy and cold, unchanged
For ever, both in kind and in degree.
Large hail, discolor'd water, sleety flaw
Through the dun midnight air stream'd down amain:
Stank all the land whereon that tempest fell.

Cerberus, cruel monster, fierce and strange,
Through his wide threefold throat, barks as a dog
Over the multitude immersed beneath.
His eyes glare crimson, black his unctuous beard,
His belly large, and claw'd the hands, with which
He tears the spirits, flays them, and their limbs
Piecemeal disparts. Howling there spread, as curs,
Under the rainy deluge, with one side
The other screening, oft they roll them round,

A wretched, godless crew. When that great worm
Descried us, savage Cerberus, he oped
His jaws, and the fangs show'd us; not a limb
Of him but trembled. Then my guide, his palms
Expanding on the ground, thence fill'd with earth
Raised them, and cast it in his ravenous maw.
E'en as a dog, when the morsel comes, lests fall
His fury, bent alone with eager hasted
To swallow it; so dropp'd the loathsome cheeks
Of demon Cerberus, who thundering stuns
The spirits, that they for deafness wish in vain.

## The Poet

Dante is the major Italian poet of the Late Middle Ages, most celebrated for his masterpiece, **The Divine Comedy**. Significantly, Dante went against poetic convention by writing in contemporary Italian, rather than Latin, setting a precedent for future poets. **The Divine Comedy** depicts the poet's journey through the realms of hell, purgatory and paradise, accompanied by the Roman poet Virgil and Dante's beloved Beatrice who act as his guides. Charting the poet's spiritual journey, **The Divine Comedy** is an autobiographical allegory peopled with characters from Dante's life.

## The Poem

Written in a three-line stanza form with an interlocking rhyme pattern known as terza rima[1] [aba, bcb, cdc etc.] which Dante invented, **The Divine Comedy** is a hugely influential epic narrative. In this extract from Book 1, 'Inferno', Canto VI, the poet has been travelling through the various circles of hell towards the innermost circle where the worst sinners are punished. Here he arrives at the third circle and happens upon the three-headed dog Cerberus, a familiar monster for Harry Potter fans.

What would we imagine the weather to be like in Hell? Dante's setting establishes a miserable, wintery atmosphere. The poet piles up adjectives ['ceaseless...unchanged'] and employs sensual imagery, mixing visual and tactile descriptions. This is a place of relentless 'showers', 'hail' and 'sleet'. The tempestuous weather is an emblem of the disorder that characterises Hell. Despite the light, the atmosphere is suitably gloomy ['dun'] and 'cold'. Moral rottenness is implied the visual image of discolouration and the olfactory one of the place: 'stank all the land'.

This is the gloomy backdrop for the main focus of the passage, the three-headed, dog-man hybrid 'demon' Cerberus. Visual imagery focuses on the monstrous parts of Cerberus' body; his 'crimson eyes' suggest fury; his 'beard' is ominously 'black'; his 'hands' [now paws] are 'claw'd'. Dante also catalogues dangerous parts of the creature, its 'jaws' and 'fangs' and 'maw'.

---

[1] The translator of this version of The Divine Comedy has used a form of blank verse rather than terza rima.

Cerberus makes a horrible 'thundering' noise and with 'ravenous' appetite inflicts savage torture on the damned as the verbs 'tears' and 'flays' emphasise. The terrible effect of his violence is also registered by the 'howling' of his victims.

## The Teaching Ideas

➜    Younger pupils and/or those skilled in art might like to draw Cerberus or turn this visually rich, filmic passage into graphic novel form. Famously **The Divine Comedy** has been illustrated by the French artist Gustave Dore [1832-1883], whose pictures of Cerberus pupils might research.

➜  What are the key features of a really memorable monster? What other monsters do pupils know from literary stories? The minotaur, vampires, dragons, the kraken, Grendel, witches, ogres, daleks etc. See how many they can list. From the list you should be able to identify some common characteristics.

➜    In my experience, pupils nearly always enjoy the opportunity to invent their own new monsters. Either they can draw a monster and label its most horrendous features, or, older or more ambitious, pupils could write a description in prose or poetic form. Whichever writing task they choose, pupils should try to create a close-up picture and have a sense of themselves as observers of the monster. At the end of their description pupils could follow Dante's example and describe what happens when the monster turns and faces them. You could come back to this work when reading Lewis Carroll's *Jabberwocky* which, of course, features another famously beastly critter.

# Geoffrey Chaucer [1343 -1400]

## Extract from *The Prologue to The Canterbury Tales*

The Miller was a stout carl, for the nones,
Ful big he was of braun, and eek of bones
That proved wel, for over-all he cam,
At wrastling he wolde have alwey the ram.
He was short-sholdred, brood, a thikke knarre,
There was no dore he nolde heve of harre
Or breke it, at a renning, with his heed.
His berd as any sowe or fox was reed,
And ther-to brood, as though it were a spade.
Upon the cop right of his nose he hade
A werte, and theron stood a toft of herys
Reed as the bristles of a sowes eres,
His nose-thirles blake were and wyde.
A swerd and bokelet bar he by his syde;
His mouth as greet as a greet forneys.
He was a janglere and a goliardeys,
And that was most of sinne and harlotyres
Wel coude he stelen corn, and tolled thryes
And yet he hadde a thombe of gold, pardee.
A whyt cote and a blew hood wered he.
A baggepype wel coude he blowe and sowne
And therwithal he broghte us out of towne.

## The Poet

Considered to the 'father' of English Literature, Geoffrey Chaucer was a courtier, diplomat and civil servant during the Middle Ages. Chaucer's most famous work is the enormously influential **The Canterbury Tales** and its prologue, from which this portrait comes. In this work each pilgrim on their journey to Canterbury takes a turn to tell a story to entertain the rest of the group. Often the stories are as revealing about their teller as they are about the events they depict. Unsurprisingly the miller tells a bawdy comic story. Clearly Chaucer was appreciated in his own time as, for his services, Edward III granted the poet the provision of 'a galon of wine daily for the rest of his life'.

## The Poem

Millers earned their living from grinding corn in windmills, hard physical work that made them tough nuts. Chaucer's sharp-eyed, satirical portrait of the miller, written in elegantly rhyming couplets, concentrates on this character's rough physicality. Certainly the miller is far more brawn than brain. Even when he does employ the latter it is through using his head to bash down doors. The miller is 'stout', 'ful byg' both of bone and of 'brawn'. 'Short', his physique is 'broad' and 'thikke'. He's strong too, being able to heave doors off their hinges [for whatever reason].

The miller's face is well-matched to his thickset body; he has a 'greet' large mouth [both physically and symbolically], 'wyde' nostrils, a 'brood' black beard and a wart with a tufy of red hair. Ominously, red and black are his dominant colours. A series of similes comparing his features to a furnace, a sow and a fox suggest danger and ugliness, but also cunning. Presumably he uses the latter in his cheating his customers, from which he makes a tidy profit; 'he hadde a thombe of gold', as Chaucer caustically puts it.

## The Teaching Ideas

Chaucer's language, Middle English, is almost 700 years old. It would be remarkable if we could read it without any difficulty. And, naturally, pupils are likely to focus on the words and phrases they don't recognise or understand. Hearing the extract read out well really can aid understanding. If you know Middle English you'll read it yourself If you're not familiar with it, a good rule of thumb is that most syllables are pronounced, hence 'eyres' is pronounced 'ear' + 'ezz', i.e. ears. There are recordings and DVDs available online.

In fact, we can understand a huge amount of this portrait without too much trouble.

➜ Emphasise this by writing the first two lines up a board and underlining all the words we can recognise. Of the nineteen words only three are unfamiliar, 'nones', 'carl' and 'eek' and they don't really get the way of the gist of the lines. 'For the nones' is a phrase meaning something along the lines of 'for the occasion'. Pupils may be able to guess that 'carl' means ordinary bloke, or churl, and 'eek' means also. Give the meaning of 'goliardeys' [coarse buffoon] and some other words, if they like. Now they can go through the rest of the poem, working in pairs, underlining the words they already know and/ or can decipher with some strenuous effort, such as 'wrastlyng' and 'forneys'. Help them to whatever degree you deem necessary, but make them do at least some the linguistic detective work.

➜ Now they can have a go at writing their modern translation. You might drop in clues, such as the fact that 'rams' were, apparently, prizes at wrestling competition and calling someone a 'janglere' was obviously insulting. Around ten teacher minutes should be enough. Once you've shared a few versions, show them a modern one:

> The MILLER was a stout fellow indeed;
> He was very strong of muscle, and also of bones.
> That was well proven, for wherever he came,
> At wrestling he would always take the prize.
> He was stoutly built, broad, a large-framed fellow;
> There was no door that he would not heave off its hinges,
> Or break it by running at it with his head.
> His beard was red as any sow or fox,
> And moreover broad, as though it were a spade.
> Upon the exact top of his nose he had
>
> A wart, and thereon stood a tuft of hairs,

Red as the bristles of a sow's ears;
His nostrils were black and wide.
He wore a sword and a buckler by his side.
His mouth was as large as a large furnace.
He was a loudmouth and a buffoon,
And that was mostly of sin and deeds of harlotry.
He well knew how to steal corn and take payment three
times;
And yet he had a thumb of gold, indeed.
He wore a white coat and a blue hood.
He well knew how to blow and play a bag-pipe,
And with that he brought us out of town.


➔    Older pupils could research the tale the miller tells, though, as you may
know, this is rather ribald. All ages of pupils might enjoy drawing the miller
and labelling their illustrations with his various features.  They could compare
their version with how the miller appears in the animated recordings, which
are available on DVD.

# Thomas Sackville, Earl of Dorset [1536 - 1608]

## *Extract from A Myrroure for Magistrates*

Lastly stood War, in glittering arms yclad,
With visage grim, stern looks, and blackly hu'd;
In his right hand a naked sword he had,
That to the hilts was all with blood imbru'd;
And in his left, that kings and kingdoms ru'd,
Famine and fire he held, and therewithal
He razed towns and threw down towers and all.

Cities he sack'd and realms, that whilom flower'd
In honour, glory, and rule above the best,
He overwhelm'd and all their fame devour'd,
Consum'd, destroy'd, wasted, and never ceas'd,
Till he their wealth, their name, and all oppress'd;
His face forhew'd with wounds, and by his side
There hung his targe, with gashes deep and wide.

# The Poet

Writer, knight, diplomat and chancellor of Oxford University, Thomas Sackville was the co-author of the first English play to be written in blank verse. He is often credited for being the driving force behind the anthology of poems that is *A Myrroure for Magistrates*. More certainly, his contributions are superior to those of his fellow co-authors.

# The Poem

Sackville personifies war as mixture between a scarred army veteran, with his 'wounds' and 'gashes' and an awesome, though mindlessly destructive, god. Visual imagery conveys War's implacable grim looks and character: He, and here War is personified as male, may be clad in 'glittering arms', but he is 'grim' and 'stern' and 'black hu'd'. This figure is clearly dangerous; his sword is unsheathed, ready for action ['naked'] and, in a grisly detail, it is covered with blood up 'to the hilts'. The monumental scale of War is implied by his holding of 'fire' and 'famine' in his hands and by the fact that working alone he 'razed' and 'threw down' and 'sack'd' towns, towers and cities.

Sackville doesn't offer any psychology or motivation behind War's actions. War is hell-bent on destruction seemingly for its own sake. The poet suggest that destruction is a kind of insatiable appetite as cities are 'devour'd'. The brutally of that verb is emphasised through contrast with its rhyme word which had described cities as having metaphorically 'flower'd', before War entered the scene. The emotional heart of the poet is the run of verbs in the middle of the second stanza, an appalling list of pitiless, unstoppable destruction 'devour'd / Consum'd, destroy'd, wasted, and never ceas'd'.

# The Teaching Ideas

It's good, I think, to start some lessons off in an unexpected way.

➜ As your class enter your room have Holst's God of War playing as loudly as you dare or your colleagues will allow. Once the class are seated, pause the music, and ask the pupils to write down any thoughts, images or emotions that come to mind as they listen to a couple of minutes of the music. What do they think the music might be describing? Now play them a couple of minutes or so of God of War from the PlayStation game:

https://www.youtube.com/watch?v=Of3hLWsBCLs. What do the two pieces of music have in common? Hopefully they will appreciate how the modern music is a kind of update of Holst's.

➜   So, now their task is to update the depiction of war.
They have two options:

1.   Re-write the portrait of war as a modern, twenty-first century figure
2.   Re-write the portrait of war as a female figure.

Either they can write their descriptions in prose or, if you or they are ambitious, they can try poetry, following Sackville's two seven-line stanza pattern, rhyming ABABBCC, a pattern known as rhyme royal.

➜   The Greeks had two war gods, the male god Ares and female one, Athena, and the Romans had the war god, Mars. What different roles did these gods perform in war? Pupils might enjoy researching war gods from other cultures...

# Edmund Spenser [1552 - 1599}

## *Extract from The Fairie Queene*

And by his side rode loathsome Gluttony,
Deformed Creature, on a filthy Swine,
His Belly was up-blown with Luxury,
And eke with Fatness swollen were his eyne:
And like a Crane, his Neck was long and fine,
With which he swallowed up excessive Feast,
For want whereof poor People oft did pine;
And all the way, most like a brutish Beast,
He spewed up his Gorge that all did him detest.

In green Vine Leaves he was right fitly clad,
For other Clothes he could not wear for Heat;
And on his Head an Ivy Garland had,
From under which fast trickled down the Sweat:

Still as he rode, he some-what still did eat,
And in his Hand did bear a Bouzing-Can,
Of which he supt so oft, that on his Seat
His drunken Corse he scarce upholden can;
In Shape and Life, more like a Monster than a Man.

## The Poet

From humble beginnings as the son of a weaver Edmund Spenser rose to become one of the foremost poets of the Elizabethan age. Despite his background, Spenser did not lack for ambition, setting out in **The Fairie Queene** to write the first English epic and to glorify Queen Elizabeth. Spenser also hoped that reading his epic would turn his readers into noblemen.

## The Poem

**The Fairie Queene** dramatises the journeys of several knights who are tested morally by their various experiences along the way. The extract features another personification, this time the sin, Gluttony. The portrait is presented in a similar way to Sackville's personification of War, with the character framed in a static pose, as if in a painting. Disgust is the main response Spenser wants to generate in the reader: Gluttony is 'loathsome', 'deformed' and sits on a suitably 'filthy swine'; his 'belly' is 'upblown' and even his eyes are 'swollen' with 'fatness'; his long non-human neck allows him to gulp down food and he's constantly overheated and sweaty. As he rides along, he drunkenly sways, while swigging from a 'bouzing can' and also somehow managing to guzzle food down too. One small wafer-thin mint more and you'd think he'd pop.

## The Teaching Ideas

The deadly sins are introduced in a parade in Book 1 of Spenser's fantastical Elizabethan Epic. They are advisers, the 'six sage counsellors' of their Queen, Pride. Each sin rides on an appropriate beast: 'Idleness' rides a 'slothful ass'; Avarice rides a 'camel loaden all with gold'. Which of the deadly sins might ride a 'ravenous wolf'?

→   Pupils should pick a deadly sin, and describe in two lines a suitable beast to carry him or her. Read out these descriptions for the rest of the class to guess the sin from the beast.

→   Match the sin to its beast; they've been muddled up in this grid. The correct matching can be found at the back of this book on page 185.

| SIN | BEAST |
|---|---|
| Idleness | A ravenous wolf |
| Avarice | A lion, loth to be lead |
| Gluttony | A slothful ass |
| Lechery | A camel, loaden all with gold |
| Wrath | A coach, adorned all with gold and garlands |
| Pride | A filthy swine |
| Envy | A bearded goat |

→ Read out the following description. Which sin is this?

And him besides rides fierce revenging ........,
Upon a Lion, loth for to be led;
And in his Hand a burning Brond he hath,
The which he brandisheth about his Head;
His Eyes did hurle forth Sparkles fiery red,
And stared stern on all that him beheld,
As Ashes pale of hew and seeming dead;
And on his Dagger still his Hand he held;
Trembling through hasty Rage, when Choler in him swell'd.

Your pupils may have noticed that each portrait of a personified sin is the same length in lines: one stanza, nine lines long. Closer inspection will reveal that both stanzas also follow the same rhyme: ABABBCBCC. In fact, this nine line stanza with its intermeshed rhyme scheme is now called the Spenserian Stanza.

→ Knowing that this is the pattern, pupils should be able to make a good stab at filling in the blanks from the following stanzas which describes Wrath in greater detail:

His ruffin Raiment all was stain'd with .........
Which he had spilt, and all to Rags ............,
Through unadvised Rashness woxen wood;

For of his Hands he had no government,
Ne car'd for Blood in his avengement:
But when the ............. Fit was overpast,
His ........... Facts he often would ....................;
Yet wilful Man he never would forecast,
How many Mischiefs should ensue his heedless hast.

➜ Pupils could take one of Spenser's portraits and modernise it or choose another abstract concept and personify it. The description can be in prose, or for the ambitious in a Spenserian Stanza. Here are some suggestions: Famine, Virtue, Kindness, Vanity...

# Christopher Marlowe [1564-1593]

## *The Passionate Shepherd to his Love*

Come live with me and be my love,
And we will all the pleasures prove,
That Valleys, groves, hills, and fields,
Woods, or steepy mountain yields.

And we will sit upon the Rocks,
Seeing the Shepherds feed their flocks,
By shallow Rivers to whose falls
Melodious birds sing Madrigals.

And I will make thee beds of Roses
And a thousand fragrant posies,
A cap of flowers, and a kirtle
Embroidered all with leaves of Myrtle;

A gown made of the finest wool
Which from our pretty Lambs we pull;
Fair lined slippers for the cold,

With buckles of the purest gold;

A belt of straw and Ivy buds,
With Coral clasps and Amber studs:
And if these pleasures may thee move,
Come live with me, and be my love.

The Shepherds' Swains shall dance and sing
For thy delight each May-morning:
If these delights thy mind may move,
Then live with me, and be my love.

## The Poet

Shakespeare's premier rival for the crown of greatest playwright of the age, writer of **Doctor Faustus**, **Tamburlaine the Great** and **The Jew of Malta**, the brilliant bad boy of Elizabethan literature, Christopher 'Kit' Marlow was killed, aged just twenty-nine, in a pub in Deptford, stabbed in the eye during an altercation by a love rival. Or was he? Scholars believe Marlowe may have been a government spy, a secret agent, and that his untimely murder was, in fact, connected to his espionage work. Some scholars even believe Marlowe's death was staged and that actually he was smuggled abroad, writing plays and sending them to one W. Shakespeare to publish under his name.

## The Poem

What would be the reality of the work of a shepherd in the C16th do you suppose? My guess is that it might be rather hard work, especially in the winter time. The speaker of Marlowe's famous pastoral love song does a good job of making his offer sound attractive, don't you think? This woman only has to consent to be his love and a rich life of endless pleasure, leisure and luxury will be hers. A little flower symbolism hints at both passionate love ['roses'] and constancy/ faithfulness 'myrtle']. Only a cynic would wonder how this shepherd could conjure wild birds to sing 'madigrals' and afford to give presents made of 'finest wool', 'purest gold', coral and amber. The belt of 'straw and Ivy buds' sounds a bit more realistic.

Written in effortless couplet rhymes with a regular, sonorous tetrameter and a gently insistent, lilting refrain, the easy, unforced mellifluous of Marlowe's poem embodies the best of the shepherd's offer. Who, indeed, could resist such honey-tongued wooing?

## The Teaching Ideas

Marlowe's poem places the reader in the position of the beloved. If this amorous poem were addressed to you specifically would it persuade you to go and be Marlowe's shepherd's love? If not, why not? How does the poet try to persuade his listener? What might be modern equivalents of the shepherd's love gifts?

➡ Pupils could modernise the poem, writing in the voice of an amorous computer programmer or garage mechanic or some such modern worker, adapting the offer to the job the speaker does. Alternatively, they could convert the poem into a lonely-hearts advert or online dating profile. They may need to be shown a few of these to get the gist of how they're written. For example, 'HAPPY-GO-LUCKY, attractive East End woman, loves keeping fit, cooking and music, WLTM charming male, 30-35, who is 100% genuine, honest and caring, for friendship possibly more.' Crikey, that last phrase!

Here's a start: 'PASSIONATE shepherd, of uncertain age...'

Or they could write a reply in letter form, beginning 'Dear amorous shepherd...'

But if those options all sound a bit too silly, more intellectual pupils could look up Sir Walter Raleigh's *The Nymph's Reply to the Shepherd*. Here's a flavour of Sir Walter's poem:

The flowers do fade, and wanton fields,
To wayward winter reckoning yields,
A honey tongue, a heart of gall,
Is fancy's spring, but sorrow's fall.

# William Shakespeare [1564-1616]

## *All the World's a Stage* (from *As You Like It*)

All the world's a stage,
And all the men and women merely players;
They have their exits and their entrances;
And one man in his time plays many parts,
His acts being seven ages. At first the infant,
Mewling and puking in the nurse's arms;
And then the whining school-boy, with his satchel
And shining morning face, creeping like snail
Unwillingly to school. And then the lover,
Sighing like furnace, with a woeful ballad
Made to his mistress' eyebrow. Then a soldier,
Full of strange oaths, and bearded like the pard,
Jealous in honour, sudden and quick in quarrel,
Seeking the bubble reputation

Even in the cannon's mouth. And then the justice,
In fair round belly with good capon lin'd,
With eyes severe and beard of formal cut,
Full of wise saws and modern instances;
And so he plays his part. The sixth age shifts
Into the lean and slipper'd pantaloon,
With spectacles on nose and pouch on side;
His youthful hose, well sav'd, a world too wide
For his shrunk shank; and his big manly voice,
Turning again toward childish treble, pipes
And whistles in his sound. Last scene of all,
That ends this strange eventful history,
Is second childishness and mere oblivion;
Sans teeth, sans eyes, sans taste, sans everything.

# Witches' Song (from *Macbeth*)

Double, double toil and trouble;

Fire burn and caldron bubble.

Fillet of a fenny snake,

In the caldron boil and bake;

Eye of newt and toe of frog,

Wool of bat and tongue of dog,

Adder's fork and blind-worm's sting,

Lizard's leg and howlet's wing,

For a charm of powerful trouble,

Like a hell-broth boil and bubble.


Double, double toil and trouble;

Fire burn and caldron bubble.

Cool it with a baboon's blood,

Then the charm is firm and good.

# Sonnet 18

Shall I compare thee to a summer's day?
Thou art more lovely and more temperate:
Rough winds do shake the darling buds of May,
And summer's lease hath all too short a date;
Sometime too hot the eye of heaven shines,
And often is his gold complexion dimm'd;
And every fair from fair sometime declines,
By chance or nature's changing course untrimm'd;
But thy eternal summer shall not fade,
Nor lose possession of that fair thou ow'st;
Nor shall death brag thou wander'st in his shade,
When in eternal lines to time thou grow'st:
So long as men can breathe or eyes can see,
So long lives this, and this gives life to thee.

## The Poet

I'm not going to write much about this Shakespeare bloke as we don't actually know a huge amount about his life. Apparently, he wrote quite a few plays, some of them really quite good, though writing 37 seems a bit needy and rather like showing-off to me. [In his defence, it's said he needed help with the later ones.] Despite all those plays, in his own Elizabethan/ Jacobean / Shakespearian times it seems William may have been more famous for his poetry. Once again the show-off mentality was much in evidence; unlike every other half-decent, enamoured and silver-tongued poet this Shakespeare guy wasn't satisfied with writing a handful of peerless sonnets, oh no, he had to go and write well over a hundred, all loosely linked into a narrative sequence, the right old clever clogs.

## The Poems

Shakespeare's theatre was, of course, called The Globe and the world is a theatre metaphor crops up in almost every play he wrote. In this version the speaker presents a rather harsh, unsentimental take on the span of a man's life. Not all babies spend the whole time 'puking' and 'mewling'. Not all soldiers are courageous out of foolhardiness or vainglorious desires. The description of old age as a series of bits failing or dropping off and ending not in the promise of resurrection, but in 'mere oblivion' is particularly bleak. Decontextualised extracts from the plays are often taken to express Shakespeare politics or philosophy. Before we extrapolate like this, we should take care to notice who speaks the lines, to whom and to what purpose. These lines, of course, are spoken by the wise fool, Jaques, and the unromantic picture is tainted by this malcontented character's world view.

The rhythm is, obviously, the most striking aspect of this spell from Macbeth. The first line sets up an emphatic, chanting beat. The effect is created by the use of trochees, so that the line starts with a stressed foot, the immediate repetition of the word 'double', alliteration of 'toil' and 'trouble', the internal rhyme and run of 'l' sounds that connect the words tightly together sonically. Around two hundred years later William Blake will echo this pattern with 'tiger, tiger, burning bright'.

Shakespeare's poem is a sonnet with a particular, English form. The whole poem develops a metaphor comparing a beloved person to a summer's day, finding the former superior to the latter in all respects. There are various points of comparison in this conceit; loveliness, climate, consistency and so forth. The really critical thing, however, is that the poem itself will allow the beloved to escape time and be immortalised, to live again each time a new reader reads it.

## The Teaching Ideas

In *All the Worlds' a Stage* the various versions of one life are presented like a parade before our eyes in rich pictorial, almost cartoonish detail.

→  This parade could be modernised, feminised, learnt by heart, performed, illustrated or perhaps story-boarded.

→  The witches' song is perfect for solo or group performances, especially for younger pupils. They also enjoy adding their own gory ingredients as extra couplets to the spell and should be encouraged to maintain the metre and rhyme scheme. 'scabby warts from an ogre's head, fungus from old mouldy bread' etc. Once they've created a few lines they can extend it into a whole new version of the spell.

→  Older pupils could consider different ways of staging, choreographing and reading the lines. Every new production of Macbeth has to escape from what have become clichéd depictions of witches. What costumes should the witches wear? How can pupils make their staging original? Once they've had a go at designing their production, they could watch and evaluate a few versions via Youtube.

→  *Shall I Compare thee...* can be used to introduce pupils to some key poetic terms and techniques. Firstly, it is, of course a sonnet. Sonnets came to England via Italy and the Petrarchan form [exemplified later in this anthology by Edna St. Vincent Millay]. Italian is easier to rhyme in, than English and English writers soon found they needed to prise open the form a little by introducing more rhymes. Shakespeare, of course, also helped develop the closing couplet which acts as a summary of the previous twelve lines. With a bright, keen group you might also introduce other technical terms to do with sonnets, such as octave, sestet, volta, iambic pentameter. Secondly, as we have noted, the whole poem is constructed on an extended metaphor, technically called a conceit.

With its conceit , fourteen lines and set  rhyme scheme, Shakespeare's sonnet has a disinct structure. This means it would lend itself well to a puzzle-solving type exercise.

➔   Give the class just the first line and then all the rest of the lines scrambled into disorder. Their task is to put it back into the correct order. If they need a little help, or you're just feeling kind, you could give them the rhyme scheme.

In Elizabethan literary culture the more improbable the two things being compared the greater the wit the poet had to demonstrate. Pupils should try to come up with as many things as possible that are nothing like love or like a beloved. Two minutes should be plenty. Gather ideas. Here are a few: a Macky D; a washing machine; a block of cement; a football team; a filing cabinet; a tin of spam.

➔    Give pupils around ten to fifteen teacher minutes to write as many lines of their sonnet as possible, beginning with the immortal, 'Shall I compare thee to a Macky D/ washing machine/ block of cement etc.'

# Robert Herrick [1591-1674]

## *To Dianeme*

SWEET, be not proud of those two eyes
Which starlike sparkle in their skies;
Nor be you proud that you can see
All hearts your captives, yours yet free;
Be you not proud of that rich hair
Which wantons with the love-sick air;
Whenas that ruby which you wear,
Sunk from the tip of your soft ear,
Will last to be a precious stone
When all your world of beauty's gone.

## The Poet

Poet, cleric and long-time country vicar, Robert Herrick, is now most famous for writing the immortal line 'gather you rosebuds while ye may' which expresses the Carpe Diem theme found in much of his poetry. Influenced by classical authors and by Ben Johnson, Herrick's work is gracefully constructed, although his focus on the female form has sometimes been frowned upon by more puritanical readers.

## The Poem

Written in couplets and in common metre [tetrameter] this is one example of many, many poems written by men flattering beautiful women and simultaneously warning them of the dangers of vanity. Clearly this woman, with his sparkly eyes, rich hair and soft ears [are soft ears attractive?] was very beautiful and was in danger of enjoying conceitedly the effect her beauty had on other people. There is something deliberately flirtatious in the way her hair even 'wantons' with the 'air'. Turning 'wanton' into a verb and personifying even the air as 'love-sick' are great touches. The poem ends with the serious and moralistic words of a vicar, the grave, sobering observation emphasised by the heavy final rhymes of 'stone' and 'gone'. Is the subtext, perhaps, that the lady ought to accept love, perhaps even that of the poem's speaker?

## The Teaching Ideas

➜   Compare and contrast this poem with Herrick's most famous one, *To the Virgins, to Make Much of Time*. How are these poems similar and how are they different? Consider tone, message and style.

➜   Compare Herrick's depiction of women with a women's depiction of themselves in either H.D. 's poem *Sea-Rose* or Millay's sonnet.

> Gather ye rosebuds while ye may,
> Old Time is still a-flying;
> And this same flower that smiles today
> Tomorrow will be dying.

The glorious lamp of heaven, the sun,
The higher he's a-getting,
The sooner will his race be run,
And nearer he's to setting.
That age is best which is the first,
When youth and blood are warmer;
But being spent, the worse, and worst
Times still succeed the former.

Then be not coy, but use your time,
And while ye may, go marry;
For having lost but once your prime,
You may forever tarry.

# John Milton [1608-1674]

## The Fallen Angels (from Paradise Lost)

Him the Almighty Power
Hurled headlong flaming from th' ethereal sky,
With hideous ruin and combustion, down
To bottomless perdition, there to dwell
In adamantine chains and penal fire,
Who durst defy th' Omnipotent to arms.
Nine times the space that measures day and night
To mortal men, he, with his horrid crew,
Lay vanquished, rolling in the fiery gulf,
Confounded, though immortal. But his doom
Reserved him to more wrath; for now the thought
Both of lost happiness and lasting pain
Torments him: round he throws his baleful eyes,
That witnessed huge affliction and dismay,
Mixed with obdurate pride and steadfast hate.
At once, as far as Angels ken, he views

The dismal situation waste and wild.
A dungeon horrible, on all sides round,
As one great furnace flamed; yet from those flames
No light; but rather darkness visible
Served only to discover sights of woe,
Regions of sorrow, doleful shades, where peace
And rest can never dwell, hope never comes
That comes to all, but torture without end
Still urges, and a fiery deluge, fed
With ever-burning sulphur unconsumed.
Such place Eternal Justice has prepared
For those rebellious; here their prison ordained
In utter darkness, and their portion set,
As far removed from God and light of Heaven
As from the centre thrice to th' utmost pole.

# The Poet

Alongside writers of the stature of Chaucer and Shakespeare, John Milton is one of the giants of the English literary canon. Politically engaged, Milton was a staunch Republican and a voluble one who openly advocated regicide. After the Restoration he was fortunate to escape execution.

Milton's most celebrated work is, of course, *Paradise Lost*, comprising twelve books of staggering scope and ambition in which the poet had the audacity to re-tell key parts of the Bible, and in the process refashion and Christianise the classical epic, with the avowed aim to 'justify the ways of God to man'. Consider too that Milton had lost his sight by this stage of his life and he dictated the blank verse lines to amanuenses and you'll get some sense of the monumental scale of the poet's achievement.

# The Poem

Re-writing critical parts of the Bible was always going to prove controversial. How could God be depicted? How could Adam and Eve be presented as fully human and yet absolutely innocent? Another key point of critical controversy has been Milton's characterisation of Satan. Since Paradise Lost was published in 1667 debate has raged over whether Milton portrayed Satan too sympathetically, almost, in fact, too heroically. Certainly, Satan seems the most vivid and dynamic character in the epic and Milton grants him several soliloquies. The Romantic poets, especially Shelley and Blake, admired Satan's rebellious character and even his doomed attempts to overthrow the absolute power of God. Indeed, Blake went so far to say that Milton's presentation of Satan is so vivid and dynamic is because he was of the 'devil's party, without knowing it'.

This extract describes in dynamic, almost cinematic visual detail Satan being thrown out of heaven and down into the dungeon of hell. The passage is chock-ful of vivid choices of language, from the opening alliteration of 'hurled headlong' to the strange, but brilliantly impossible 'darkness visible'. Milton's sinuous syntax and extensive use of enjambment also contribute to the vividness and the sense of dropping downwards. Naturally, there's a lot of fire imagery too. Are we nudged towards some sympathy for Satan? We find out what he is feeling, the 'lost happiness', see his 'baleful eyes' and words for unhappiness, 'woe', 'sorrow' and 'doleful' are thick on the ground. To modern ears 'torture without end' might sound excessive and we may wonder, too, an omniscient and omnipotent God created Satan and his 'horrid crew' in the first place.

## The Teaching Ideas

Poetry by Heart selected another extract from **Paradise Lost** and hearing it read by students was electrifying. You can find these readings at: http://www.poetrybyheart.org.uk/poems/paradise-lost-book-1-lines-242-315/ It would take an ambitious KS3 pupil to attempt to learn this section off-by-heart, but they might take inspiration from Milton's ambition in writing the epic in the first place.

Consider how sympathetic should we feel to Satan here? He's a villain, in fact, the original, arch-villain. But Milton also presents his as clever, determined, charismatic and brave.

➔     List other famous literary villains - Macbeth, Moriarty, Mrs Coulter, Voldemort etc. Or, turn this exercise into a competition: Put pupils in pairs and give them five minutes to come up with as many famous fictional villains from books and films as they can. Scoring: One point for each one they get up to 5; two points for each villain from 6 - 10; five points for 11-15; ten points for 15 +. An extra five points is available if they can name five female villains. So, if they managed to name eight villains their total would be eleven points. The teacher will adjudicate on any marginal decisions, such as whether Grabber Train from Thomas the Tank Engine should be allowed [The correct answer being no.] A list of villains can be found at the end of this section.

What features do these characters have in common? Which ones are the most compelling? Why? Which ones are the scariest? If we were creating a villain wow could we subvert readers' expectations about these types of characters?

➔     Pupils can now create their own villain. They should describe this character in one paragraph, as if they are watching him/her from close-by, but unseen, as the villain is going about doing some characteristically villainous thing. In the next paragraph they should swap perspectives. Writing from the villain's point-of-view they should describe themselves watching him or her.

➜ Satan claims it is better to rule in hell than be a servant in heaven. This could make an interesting topic for debate. In pairs, each pupil writes down as many arguments as they can think or for one side of this argument while their partner writes as many for the opposite side. Five to ten minutes preparation should be long enough. Debate in pairs and then work up to class debate with the most convincing speakers.

Emperor Palpatine

| | | | |
|---|---|---|---|
| The Joker | Sauron | Cruella de Vil | Richard III |
| Iago | Edmund | Claudius | Lady |
| Macbeth/Blofeld | Fagin | Darth Vader | Scar |
| Mrs Trunchbull | Count Olaf | Dracula | Mr Hyde |
| The White witch | Captain Hook | The Snow Queen | The Wicked |
| Witches | Alec D'Urberville | Long John Silver | Shere Khan |

# Alexander Pope [1688 - 1744]

## *Gulliver in Lilliput*

From his nose
Clouds he blows.
When he speaks,
Thunder breaks.
When he eats,
Famine threats.
When he treads
Mountains' heads
Groan and shake;
Armies quake.
See him stride
Valleys wide.
Over woods,
Over floods.
Troops take heed,
Man and steed:
Left and right,
Speed your flight!
In amaze
Lost I gaze
Towards the skies
See! And believe your eyes!

## The Poet

The sharp-tongued, quick-witted and diminutive Augustan poet, Alexander Pope is celebrated for his mastery of the heroic couplet and his employment of it in satirical verse of neo-classical elegance, most famously the mock epic, *The Rape of the Lock*. Pope's capacity to shape a memorable phrase is reflected in his well-known comment that Shakespeare expresses 'What oft was thought, but ne'er so well expressed'.

## The Poem

Pope's facility for rhyming is showcased in this slight, very tall and thin dramatic monologue written in the voice of a Lilliputian. Technically speaking the poem's written in the relatively rare dimeter, i.e. lines with only two beats, and these are composed of amphimacers [metrical feet following a stress - unstress - stress pattern]. This strict, constraining pattern is managed right up to the final lines.

## The Teaching Ideas

→ Take the title away and ask pupils to come up with possible titles. Make the task a bit more demanding by presented the poem first as prose, getting rid of some the capitalisation and with some of the rhyme words and even the odd line blanked out:

*From his nose, clouds he blows. When he speaks, thunder ........When he eats, famine threats. When he treads, mountains' ......... Groan and shake; armies ............... See him stride ............................. Over woods, over floods. Troops take heed, man and steed: Left and right, speed your flight! In .......... lost I gaze. Towards the ............... See! And believe your eyes.*

You might have to point out the stress pattern so that pupils follow it.

→ Ask them to re-arrange the words in different ways on the page. Once you've revealed the blanks, the form and the title ask them why Pope might have arranged the poem in this tower-like form.

→ Pupils could research, and perhaps even read Jonathan Swift's marvelous novel **Gulliver's Travels** in preparation for writing a poem entitled *Gulliver in Brobdingnag*. Discuss whether they should use short lines and whether the poem should be very small on the page. Here's a start: 'Tiny feet and tiny hands/ only a few inches tall he stands...'

➜     What other stories do you and/ or the pupils know about giants? There's the cyclops from **The Odyssey**, the giant who comes a cropper at the hands of Jack of beanstalk fame, Roald Dahl's BFG. Other than being fantastically tall, what other features do giants seem to share? If a witch symoblises fear of the mother figure, what might giants symbolise?

➜     Pupils could write a story in which they awake to find themselves as big as a house or one in which they shrink **Alice in Wonderland**-style down to the size of a mouse, or a story in which both happen.

➜     Older pupils might find J. G. Ballard's short story, *The Drowned Giant* thought-provoking.

# William Blake [1757-1827]

## *The Tyger*

Tyger Tyger, burning bright,
In the forests of the night;
What immortal hand or eye,
Could frame thy fearful symmetry?

In what distant deeps or skies.
Burnt the fire of thine eyes?
On what wings dare he aspire?
What the hand, dare seize the fire?

And what shoulder, & what art,
Could twist the sinews of thy heart?
And when thy heart began to beat,
What dread hand? & what dread feet?

What the hammer? what the chain,
In what furnace was thy brain?
What the anvil? what dread grasp,
Dare its deadly terrors clasp!

When the stars threw down their spears
And water'd heaven with their tears:
Did he smile his work to see?
Did he who made the Lamb make thee?

Tyger Tyger burning bright,
In the forests of the night:
What immortal hand or eye,
Dare frame thy fearful symmetry?

## The Poet

Visionary Romantic poet and artist William Blake was a true radical. Religiously non-conformist, ardently pro the French Revolution, Blake produced poetry and artwork that was radical both in terms of its political and philosophical content and in terms of its inimical, bold-outlined style. Blake wrote, etched, illustrated and even printed his unique poems on his own printing press at the back of his small house in Soho. Contemporary artists and writers thought the poet might be mad, but that his work was useful to copy from. Sadly, like many artists ahead of his time, Blake's work wasn't really appreciated until after his death. Look at Blake's artwork or read one of his poems and it's immediately obvious it's by him, so striking and original was his style.

## The Poem

The rhythm of the opeing lines is similar to that employed by Shakespeare in the witches' chant from Macbeth [stressed syllables are in bold]:

**Tiger, tiger burning bright**

Double, **double, toil** and **trouble**

In both examples the line begins with a double, the first word repeated immediately. In both, the stress pattern is trochaic, so that the first sound in each line is stressed. Both are also written in common metre, technically called tetrameter. In both, sonic concentration is achieved by further repetitions of sounds. In Blake's poem assonance [tiger & bright] replaces Shakespeare's full rhyme and like Shakespeare, Blake uses alliteration as well as a dominant running sound, in his case the appropriate 'rrr' sound. If anything, with the last syllable docked, Blake's line is more dynamic, more muscular and more concentrated.

The music of the poem is generated through the interaction of the metre with the sounds of the words themselves. To highlight this fact, compare 'twinkle, twinkle little star' which has an identical metre, but sounds rather different!

# The Teaching Ideas

The most immediately striking things about Blake's poem are the pulsating rhythm and the vivid imagery. The combination makes *The Tyger* an ideal poem to learn by heart and/or perform in a group. Pupils should be encouraged to use choral as well as single voices, to really emphasise the pulsating rhytm, to vary pitch, volume, pacing and so forth. Play with the variables, turn this up and that down, think of the poem as being like a piece of music and the reading as a mini-concert for voices.

➜  Older pupils should be able to answer an essay style question about how Blake makes the poem so vivid and dynamic. They may, however, benefit from scaffolding. A useful, incisive and empowering way to do this is to ask pupils to pick out five words or phrases they find particularly effective/ surprising or puzzling and to write a few sentences about each one. A word like 'symmetry', for instance, seems to come from a different linguistic world to most of the rest of the poem and prompts the question how is a tiger symmetrical in any way? Share and discuss the bits of the poem they pick out. More systematically, draw their attention to:

- the fire and industrial imagery
- the use of vivid contrasts
- the close repetition of words and phrases
- the metre, rhythm and sounds of the words

➜  Ask them to consider these statements about Blake's poem and to rank them in order of how much they agree or disagree with them:

1. Blake's poem is a vivid depiction of a beautiful, but deadly predator
2. The tiger has devilish and monstrous qualities
3. Blake's poem is really about the industrial revolution
4. Blake's poem is really more about the nature of God.

➜  In the poem Blake asks a barrage of questions culminating in asking whether the same creator could possibly have made both the lamb [a symbol for Christ, of course] as well as this fearsome, dreadful tiger. In the pupils' opinions, what is the correct answer to this question?

59

# Robert Burns [1759 - 1796]

## *To a Mouse*

Wee, sleekit[2], cowran, tim'rous beastie,
O, what a panic's in thy breastie!
Thou need na start awa sae hasty,
Wi' bickering brattle!
I wad be laith to rin an' chase thee,
Wi' murd'ring pattle!

I'm truly sorry Man's dominion
Has broken Nature's social union,
An' justifies that ill opinion,
Which makes thee startle,
At me, thy poor, earth-born companion,
An' fellow-mortal!

I doubt na, whyles, but thou may thieve;
What then? poor beastie, thou maun live!
A daimen-icker in a thrave 'S a sma' request[3]:
I'll get a blessin wi' the lave,
An' never miss't!

Thy wee-bit housie, too, in ruin!
It's silly wa's the win's are strewin!
An' naething, now, to big a new ane,
O' foggage green!
An' bleak December's winds ensuin,
Baith snell an' keen!

Thou saw the fields laid bare an' wast,
An' weary Winter comin fast,

---

2 sleek
3 an odd ear in 24 sheaves

An' cozie here, beneath the blast,
Thou thought to dwell,
Till crash! the cruel coulter[4] past
Out thro' thy cell.

That wee-bit heap o' leaves an' stibble,
Has cost thee monie a weary nibble!
Now thou's turn'd out, for a' thy trouble,
But house or hald.
To thole the Winter's sleety dribble,
An' cranreuch[5] cauld!

But Mousie, thou are no thy-lane,
In proving foresight may be vain:
The best laid schemes o' Mice an' Men,
Gang aft agley,
An' lea'e us nought but grief an' pain,
For promis'd joy!

Still, thou art blest, compar'd wi' me!
The present only toucheth thee:
But Och! I backward cast my e'e,
On prospects drear!
An' forward, tho' I canna see,
I guess an' fear!

---

[4] plough
[5] frost

61

## The Poet

The national poet of Scotland, regularly chosen by polls as the greatest Scot ever to have lived, Robert Burns, dubbed the ploughman poet, was born into a humble farming family, but acquired literary fame by the tender age of just twenty-seven. The passions of Burns' short life seem to have been Scotland and its culture [he toured Scotland, collected and wrote Scottish folk songs], women [he had several relationships], drink [he liked a good time] and song [ditto]. His most famous work is, of course, *Auld Lang Syne* which is sung lustily every New Year in Scotland and elsewhere.

## The Poem

Diction is a term for the vocabulary used in poetry. Traditionally poetic diction distinguished itself from ordinary, everyday, common language by being heightened in some way. Traditionally there were rarefied poetic words, such as 'ethereal' and 'enwrought' and non-poetic words, such as 'screwdriver' and 'went''. Traditionally the diction of English poetry was an elevated form of Standard English. Phonetically spelt, liberally using dialect words, Burns' poem sticks two fingers up at standardising conventions and uses instead the poet's rich, expressive native voice of Scots. Why the hell should a poem be written in Standard English anyway? Why should poetic language be bleached of its local colour to fit some standard form imposed by those with authority from England? Why, indeed.

Romantic poems often come from the heart and have, or seek to have, an emotional impact. Politically Romantic poems often expressed sympathy for the oppressed and presented nature as a moral force. Burns' poem is typical of the genre in expressing tender-hearted fellow feeling for a small, vulnerable animal that can do little to protect itself or its young from huge external forces, in this case the farmer's plough, despite 'nature's social union'.

## The Teaching Ideas

→ Before reading the whole poem give the class a few lines to decode. Tell them the lines are written in Scots, that the words are spelt phonetically and that some may be dialect words. Working in pairs for a couple of teacher minutes should be long enough:

- Wee, sleekit, cowran, tim'rous beastie
- Wi' bickering brattle!
- Baith snell an' keen!
- It's silly wa's the win's are strewin!
- The best laid schemes o' Mice an' Men/ Gang aft agley

Feedback ideas for what the lines might mean, but don't reveal a 'correct' translation at this stage.

This is a poem that demands to be read out loud, in a Scottish accent.

→ Taking one stanza each and alternating, pairs of pupils could have a go at speaking the lines to each other. The most confident/ best readers can then read the poem to the class. Naturally pupils often fixate on bits of poems they don't understand. Sometimes getting the gist is good enough. Moreover, developing an overall sense of what a poem's about helps to decipher micro details of words, phrases and imagery.

→ Once the poem's been read through a few times ask your pupils to summarise its content in one prose paragraph. If you feel they need more help you can find many recordings of the poem online to listen to.

Now they can examine the poem more carefully.

→ Which words or lines are hardest to decipher? Return to the words and phrases picked out at the start of the lesson, i.e. 'Wee, sleekit, cowran, tim'rous beastie' and the other four quotes. Pupils can either stick with their original translations of these or modify them now they know and understand the context. Share ideas with the rest of the class and establish a consensus about meaning.

→     Consider why anyone in their right mind would want to read the poem in Scots, when it could simply be translated into Standard English and be made much easier to understand? Discuss what might lost as well as gained by translating and standardising Burns' poem in this way.

# Samuel Taylor Coleridge [1772-1834]

## Extracts from The Rime of the Ancient Mariner

### Extract 1

Down dropt the breeze, the sails dropt down,
'Twas sad as sad could be;
And we did speak only to break
The silence of the sea!

All in a hot and copper sky,
The bloody Sun, at noon,

Right up above the mast did stand,
No bigger than the Moon.
Day after day, day after day,
We stuck, nor breath nor motion;
As idle as a painted ship
Upon a painted ocean.

Water, water, every where,
And all the boards did shrink;
Water, water, every where,
Nor any drop to drink.

The very deep did rot: O Christ!
That ever this should be!
Yea, slimy things did crawl with legs
Upon the slimy sea.

About, about, in reel and rout
The death-fires danced at night;
The water, like a witch's oils,
Burnt green, and blue and white.

## Extract 2

There passed a weary time. Each throat
Was parched, and glazed each eye.
A weary time! a weary time!
How glazed each weary eye,

When looking westward, I beheld
A something in the sky.

At first it seemed a little speck,
And then it seemed a mist;
It moved and moved, and took at last
A certain shape, I wist.

A speck, a mist, a shape, I wist!
And still it neared and neared:
As if it dodged a water-sprite,
It plunged and tacked and veered.

With throats unslaked, with black lips baked,
We could nor laugh nor wail;
Through utter drought all dumb we stood!
I bit my arm, I sucked the blood,
And cried, A sail! a sail!

With throats unslaked, with black lips baked,
Agape they heard me call:
Gramercy! they for joy did grin,
And all at once their breath drew in.
As they were drinking all.

See! see! (I cried) she tacks no more!
Hither to work us weal;
Without a breeze, without a tide,

She steadies with upright keel!
The western wave was all a-flame.
The day was well nigh done!
Almost upon the western wave
Rested the broad bright Sun;
When that strange shape drove suddenly
Betwixt us and the Sun.

And straight the Sun was flecked with bars,
(Heaven's Mother send us grace!)
As if through a dungeon-grate he peered
With broad and burning face.

Alas! (thought I, and my heart beat loud)
How fast she nears and nears!
Are those her sails that glance in the Sun,
Like restless gossameres?

Are those her ribs through which the Sun
Did peer, as through a grate?
And is that Woman all her crew?
Is that a DEATH? and are there two?
Is DEATH that woman's mate?

Her lips were red, her looks were free,
Her locks were yellow as gold:
Her skin was as white as leprosy,
The Night-mare LIFE-IN-DEATH was she,
Who thicks man's blood with cold.

The naked hulk alongside came,
And the twain were casting dice;
'The game is done! I've won! I've won!'
Quoth she, and whistles thrice.

The Sun's rim dips; the stars rush out;
At one stride comes the dark;

With far-heard whisper, o'er the sea,
Off shot the spectre-bark.

## The Poet

With his friend, William Wordsworth, Coleridge wrote one of the most important works of Romanticism, The Lyrical Ballads. Radical in terms of both subject matter and style, this collection of poems explored the lives and wisdom of ordinary, country folk and eschewed fancy, rarefied diction, choosing instead to employ the plain, spoken language of common men. At least, that's what Wordsworth wrote in the preface.

A famously sparkling conversationalist, Coleridge was the more mercurial character in the partnership with a greater interest in the fantastical and in philosophy. The mansion of Coleridge's mind contained many rooms, including some gloomy, darkened ones. The poet's taste for the Gothic is evident in one of his most famous poems, *The Rime of the Ancient Mariner*.

## The Extracts

Coleridge's fantastical ballad tells a seemingly allegorical story that has been interpreted in many different ways by scholars. The punishment of the mariner and torments of the ship's crew spring from a mindless and seemingly random act of violence against nature, the shooting of an albatross that seemed to have been guiding the ship. Benevolent nature transforms into the revenging spirit of nemesis. The ship is driven into new seas of strange and terrible weather before becoming becalmed and stuck on a 'lifeless ocean'. Out of the silence and stillness of sea a ship appears moving unnaturally swiftly towards them and on the ship, we soon realise, are a horrible crew.

In the first extract Coleridge creates a curious start-stop effect through slowing the natural lilt and onwards momentum of the ballad metre [composed of cross rhymed quatrains of alternating tetrameters and trimeters] through extensive use of repetition. The interaction between metre, diction and syntax generates a hypnotic effect, a sort of spell of stasis. For example, in close succession he writes ''twas sad as sad could be', 'day after day, day after day', 'a painted ship / upon a painted ocean' and two lots of 'water, water, everywhere'. Mood and atmosphere are generated through sensual imagery. Hissing sibilance complements colourful visual imagery, such as references to the 'cooper sky', 'bloody sun' and the water burning 'green and blue and white'.

Repetition is used extensively again in the second extract. Brilliantly Coleridge uses it to both slow and speed up time, so that 'a speck, a mist, a shape, I wist' conveys the mariner's growing excitement at the thought of rescue. Though the mariner may be excited by this shape, though he doesn't give away the nature of the ship Coleridge ensures the reader picks up ominous details. The mariner's ship is stuck in the doldrums so how, for example, can this new ship cross the water 'without a breeze, without a tide' and at such speed, 'how fast she nears and nears'?

The portrait of Life-in-Death and her spectre ship is chilling, ominous and mysterious. Nature now seems to be operating by different, inescapable rules, so that, for instance, day turns suddenly to night, 'at one stride comes the dark'. And it seems, nature is also now doing the bid of Life-in-Death. To find out what happens next, pupils will have to read the rest of the poem.

## The Teaching Ideas

➜   Coleridge's poem is visually and sonically bewitching and would lend itself well to graphic novel form. The artist Gustav Dore [1832 - 1883] produced captivating illustrations for the poem, some of which are included here. An alternative to storyboarding would be for pupils to choose one frame, or moment from the story and produce a colour illustration for it. This could be done with pencil and pens, or, if the technology's available with software such as photoshop.

➜   Nowadays pupils sometimes have easy access to sophisticated video editing equipment on smart phones, ipads and such like. If you fancy issuing a real challenge, how about pupils making short films based on Coleridge's poem?

➜   Beofore pupils rush off to read the rest of the poem, they could plan their own ending. The poem actually starts with the glittering-eyed ancient mariner, who has accosted an innocent wedding guest in order to tell him the story of this expedition. Only the mariner survived and, it seems, he is doomed to travel the earth telling his strange and haunting story as a form of penitence for his sins. What happened next? What might have happened to the rest of the crew? Who was Life-in-Death's mate? Why did she cast some dice? What does she mean 'she's won'? What has she won? What price might the ancient mariner had to pay in order to survive. Pupils could discuss, plan and/ or write the end of the poem.

→ Pupils willing to accept an even more demanding challenge could have a go at writing a bit of their story, perhaps a few stanzas, in rhyming ballad form. This means using quatrains with four beats in lines 1 & 3, three beats in lines 2 & 4. The rhyme scheme is abab. Good luck!

# Lord Byron [1788 - 1824]

## *The Destruction of Sennacherib*

The Assyrian came down like the wolf on the fold,
And his cohorts were gleaming in purple and gold;
And the sheen of their spears was like stars on the sea,
When the blue wave rolls nightly on deep Galilee.

Like the leaves of the forest when Summer is green,
That host with their banners at sunset were seen:
Like the leaves of the forest when Autumn hath blown,
That host on the morrow lay withered and strown.

For the Angel of Death spread his wings on the blast,
And breathed in the face of the foe as he passed;
And the eyes of the sleepers waxed deadly and chill,
And their hearts but once heaved, and for ever grew still!

And there lay the steed with his nostril all wide,
But through it there rolled not the breath of his pride;
And the foam of his gasping lay white on the turf,
And cold as the spray of the rock-beating surf.

And there lay the rider distorted and pale,
With the dew on his brow, and the rust on his mail:
And the tents were all silent, the banners alone,
The lances unlifted, the trumpet unblown.

And the widows of Ashur are loud in their wail,
And the idols are broke in the temple of Baal;
And the might of the Gentile, unsmote by the sword,
Hath melted like snow in the glance of the Lord!

# The Poet

'Mad, bad and dangerous to know' Lord George Gordon Byron was the wild child of English Romantic literature. Once dubbed the wickedest man alive, for one reason and another, Byron had to flee England and relocate to Italy with his friend Shelley and Shelley's young wife, Mary. It was on the shores of Lake Geneva in Switzerland, bored by the horrible weather and fuelled by red wine, no doubt, that Byron proposed the ghost writing competition which would lead Mary to writing her Gothic novel, **Frankenstein**, whose protagonist embodies many of the traits of what became known as the Byronic hero.

# The Poem

Byron's poem is full of bold, vibrant colours, significant similes and dramatic transitions, but it is the relentlessly pounding rhythm that really demonstrates the poet's mastery. In the first two stanzas there are references to 'purple and gold', 'blue waves' and the 'green' of the forest. The opening simile compares the Assyrians to predatory, merciless 'wolves' and their Christian adversaries to sheep in a 'fold', neatly setting up the expectation that the former are about to sweep down and ravage the latter. The impressive size of the Assyrian army is conveyed by comparing soldiers to 'leaves' in a forest, while the final simile suggests the laser-like heat of God's power; even a 'glance' is enough to make the Assyrian army melt 'like snow'. Byron uses parallel phrasing to express the suddenness with which God wipes away the Assyrian army. In one line they are massing like leaves on forest trees, in the very next line they are dead leaves 'withered and strown' across the forest floor.

*The Destruction of Sennacherib* is written in quatrains following a couplet rhyme pattern. There are four beats per line, so the metre is tetrameter. The stress pattern is a three-foot one; unstress - unstress - stress, unstress - unstress - stress. This is anapestic metre [stressed syllables are in bold]:

And the **wid**ows of **Ash**ur are **loud** in their **wail**

Why did Byron use this metre?
Because the anapestic rhythm mimics the sound of horses' galloping:

Di - di - **DUM** - di - di - **DUM** - di - di - **DUM** - di - di - **DUM**

Scan each line and you'll notice that the poet sometimes varies the metre a little, by docking an unstressed syllable and hurrying the verse along, as in the first foot of the first line, or by thickening the line and thus slowing the reader, as in the first stanza's last line. A keen class or pupil might find and examine the effect of other variations.

Of course, Byron is intent on conveying drama and excitement and the omnipotence of the Christian God. He is not interested in realism or in justifying this apparently supernatural slaughter on ethical grounds. It'd be interesting to compare the poet's account of the battle with any historical ones you could find or to think how the Assyrian version would tell things differently.

## The Teaching Idea

➜   'The Mighty Anapestic Tetrameter Challenge': How many lines of verse can pupils compose in this metre in 15 - 20 teacher minutes? They can write on any topic, but the line(s) must make sense.

**5** points for single lines, such as:
'I ran to the shops and I purchased a paper'.

**10** points for two continuous lines.

**15** points for two continuous lines that also rhyme, such as:
'the subject I like is a difficult one,
Not Physics or History, nor Mathematical sums'

**20** points for three continuous lines with the first two rhyming.

**30** points for a full quatrain with couplet rhymes that also makes sense.

**40** points for a full quatrain in which the subject suits the metre. Teacher's judgement of this is unquestionable and final. [I'd have provided examples of a 40 pointer, but that would just have been showing-off, of course.]

# Percy Bysshe Shelley [1792-1822]

## *Ozymandias*

I met a traveller from an antique land,
Who said -"Two vast and trunkless legs of stone
Stand in the desert. . . . Near them, on the sand,
Half sunk a shattered visage lies, whose frown,
And wrinkled lip, and sneer of cold command,
Tell that its sculptor well those passions read
Which yet survive, stamped on these lifeless things,
The hand that mocked them, and the heart that fed;
And on the pedestal, these words appear:
My name is Ozymandias, King of Kings;
Look on my Works, ye Mighty, and despair!
Nothing beside remains. Round the decay
Of that colossal Wreck, boundless and bare
The lone and level sands stretch far away."

## The Poet

Friend of Byron, husband to Mary, during his short life the idealistic, rebellious and restless Romantic poet Percy Bysshe Shelley often got himself into spots of bother. Before leaving his school Shelley blew up a tree with gunpowder for a prank. Later, having apparently only ever attended one lecture, he was thrown out of Oxford University for writing a pamphlet on the necessity of atheism. Eloping with a sixteen-year-old Mary to Italy, while still married to another woman, who was pregnant with his son, also didn't go down well with everyone, including Mary's father, the philosopher William Godwin. In his lifetime publishers were reluctant to publish Shelley's work, afraid they would be prosecuted for indecency, blasphemy, sedition or worse. But after his premature death from drowning, Shelley's poetic reputation and iconic status as someone who burnt brightly and fiercely grew, so much as that he is now considered one of the greatest and most radical of the Romantic poets.

## The Poem

Shelley's sonnet is a warning to mankind in general and to the most powerful in particular. A warning of our puniness before the enormous scale of time and nature. The hubristic, tyrannical Ozymandias might have believed his power and prestige would last forever, but all that is left is this smashed monument surrounded by barren desert. 'Nothing beside remains'. Ozymandias' self-deluding vanity is underlined by the ironic ring of the words on his pedestal: 'Look on my works, ye mighty, and despair'. Even the greatest despots cannot escape the levelling forces of nature and of time.

## The Teaching Ideas

→    Shelley's poem crops up often in GCSE specifications, so there's plenty of time then to analyse it closely. For KS3, I suggest it's a poem that can easily be learnt by heart and recited.

→    With its sonnet form and carefully linked, embedded narrative *Ozymandias* lends itself well to a sequencing exercise. Give the pupils the first line and the rest of the lines in scrambled order. Which lines could logically follow the first? Possibly the tenth, but none of the others would make any sense. The speech marks in line two are a clue and clearly this traveller is describing a statue. A few lines could possibly follow this one, 5, 6, 7, 8, at a push. Give the class a time limit, perhaps ten teacher minutes.

➜   A key idea about poetry to try to get over to pupils is that it's all about economy; using the fewest words to the greatest effect. A good poem must have no superfluous words or padding. A fun way of conveying this is by telling your class you have added a few words of your own to a poem and they need to detect these.

> I met an old traveller from an antique land,
> Who said -"Two vast and trunkless legs of stone
> Stand in the desert. . . . Near them, on the sand,
> Half sunk a shattered visage lies, whose frown,
> And wrinkled lip, and harsh sneer of cold command,
> Tell that its sculptor well those passions read
> Which yet still survive, stamped on these lifeless things,
> The hand that mocked them, and the heart that fed;
> And on the huge pedestal, these words appear:
> My name is Ozymandias, King of Kings;
> Look on my Works, ye Mighty, and despair!
> Nothing beside remains at all. Round the decay
> Of that colossal Wreck, boundless, flat and bare
> The lone and level sands stretch so far away."

➜   No harm in encouraging ambitious writers to have a go at writing a sonnet. Shelley's is a weird hybrid of sonnet forms and perhaps it would be easier to write one that follows the Shakespearian structure we came across earlier in this book. When I say easier, I mean relatively speaking...

# John Clare [1793-1864]

## *I am*

I am—yet what I am none cares or knows;
My friends forsake me like a memory lost:
I am the self-consumer of my woes—
They rise and vanish in oblivious host,
Like shadows in love's frenzied stifled throes
And yet I am, and live—like vapours tossed

Into the nothingness of scorn and noise,
Into the living sea of waking dreams,
Where there is neither sense of life or joys,
But the vast shipwreck of my life's esteems;
Even the dearest that I loved the best
Are strange—nay, rather, stranger than the rest.

I long for scenes where man hath never trod
A place where woman never smiled or wept
There to abide with my Creator, God,
And sleep as I in childhood sweetly slept,
Untroubling and untroubled where I lie
The grass below—above the vaulted sky.

# The Poet

Like Robert Burns, John Clare was born into the labouring classes and, though he achieved some literary recognition in his lifetime, Clare was also patronised as a 'peasant poet'. Clare's particular brilliance was the fine-eye for detail that helped to write vivid descriptions of nature and the countryside, often using richly expressive dialect words. But there is another parallel strain in his poetry, poems that express an uncertain, tormented sense of identity, such as *I am*. Tragically, the tender sensitivity and instability of Clare's character led him to being incarcerated in an asylum. Though Clare's personality seemed to collapse into various characters [sometimes he believed himself to be Lord Byron at other times a prize fighter] he continued to write lucidly in verse. The story of Clare's life in Dr. Matthew Allen's private asylum in Epping Forest, and his temporary escape from it, is told with great skill and empathy in Adam Foulds' novel **The Quickening Maze**.

# The Poem

It's a very powerful, very poignant poem, isn't it? A cry of loneliness, alienation, almost existential angst, and despair. Clare's simile describing the dissolution of the self is unforgettable; he lives 'like vapours tossed / into the nothingness of scorn and noise'. There's a faint echo here, I think, of Macbeth's 'full of sound and fury, signifying nothing'. Then there's the central metaphor of the 'vast shipwreck' of his 'life's esteems', the despair that even those he loves 'dearest' seem the most 'strange' and remote from him, the simple wish to return to untroubled repose - 'and sleep as I in childhood slept' - and a desire for peace and union with God that also seems a desire for death.

And yet, though, the poem certainly expresses despair it stands itself as testament to the counter-forces of the will and creative intelligence. Take, for example, the way Clare makes us hit the heartless verb 'tossed' a little harder through the surprising triple rhyme and how, by placing the word at the end of the line and of the stanza and by using enjambment, he creates a visual sense of dropping into nothingness. Or take the way the stanzas are arranged solidly, how the rhyme scheme is managed and we can begin to see the appeal of writing verse to Clare; whatever the sentiment he was expressing, poetry was the space in which he felt most fully himself, most lucid, most in control.

## The Teaching Ideas

➔      Ask pupils to pick out the five lines from the poem they find the most powerful and expressive. Once they've made their selection they then can write a few sentences about why they made their choices, trying to rank the lines 1 to 5, strongest first. Next, they compare their selection with a partner. Feedback as a class should lead to interesting discussion with the aim to reach a consensus about the most powerful lines.


➔      Every now and then I try to give pupils an unstructured, free writing task. Essentially, they can write what they like for ten minutes or so, but it must in some way be a response to whatever stimulus they have been given. It's vital that the pupils decide whether they want to share what they produce with me, or the rest of the class, or not. Tell them too that this work will not be 'assessed' using standard marking criteria. My instinct is that a poem such as Clare's *I am* might illicit some interesting and unexpected responses from pupils, if they're given space and time, and if their work is read with care and respect.

# Felicia Hemans [1793 - 1835]

## *Casabianca*

The boy stood on the burning deck,
Whence all but he had fled;
The flame that lit the battle's wreck,
Shone round him o'er the dead.
Yet beautiful and bright he stood,
As born to rule the storm;
A creature of heroic blood,
A proud, though childlike form.
The flames rolled on – he would not go,
Without his father's word;
That father, faint in death below,
His voice no longer heard.
He called aloud – 'Say, father, say
If yet my task is done?'

He knew not that the chieftain lay
Unconscious of his son.
'Speak, father!' once again he cried,
'If I may yet be gone!'
– And but the booming shots replied,
And fast the flames rolled on.
Upon his brow he felt their breath
And in his waving hair;
And look'd from that lone post of death,
In still yet brave despair.
And shouted but once more aloud,
'My father! must I stay?'
While o'er him fast, through sail and shroud,
The wreathing fires made way.
They wrapped the ship in splendour wild,
They caught the flag on high,
And streamed above the gallant child,
Like banners in the sky.
There came a burst of thunder sound –
The boy – oh! where was he?
Ask of the winds that far around
With fragments strewed the sea!
With mast, and helm, and pennon fair,
That well had borne their part,
But the noblest thing which perished there,
Was that young faithful heart.

## The Poet

The Liverpool-born, Welsh-bred, Dublin-living poet Felicia Hemans had her first poem published when she was just fourteen years old. Respected by fellow poets such as Wordsworth, Hemans' work sold well in her lifetime and remained popular in Great Britain and the USA into the mid-twentieth century. Often her poems, such as *Casabianca* were set to be learnt by heart by pupils. Having fallen out of fashion, Hemans' poetry is undergoing critical reappraisal, especially in terms of her presentation of women's lives.

## The Poem

Hemans' ballad honours and valorises the death of Giocante, son of Captain Louis de Casabianca, aboard the Orient ship during the Battle of the Nile, fought between the French and the English navies. The boy's stalwart courage is matched by his total obedience to his father as he awaits among the burning wreck for the command to abandon ship. The writer is as excited by this spectacle as she is stirred by the boy's tragic plight. The burning ship, for instance, is described as being 'wrapped' in '*splendour* wild'. For her, this immolating background makes the boy's stoicism the more noble, for despite his 'brave despair' the 'gallant' child remains on board and goes down with the ship. A 'young faithful heart' indeed.

## The Teaching Ideas

Modern readers might be less impressed by this version of doomed, self-sacrificing, seemingly futile courage than Hemans would have hoped. What is the moral we are meant to draw from the poem? In Samuel Butler's novel **The Way of All Flesh** [1903] a child extracts a rather different moral from the poem: 'young people cannot begin too soon to exercise discretion in the obedience they pay to their papa and mamma'. Well, quite.

➜     The poem could prompt a debate on the nature of honour, courage and / or the importance of obedience to parental figures. Who in the class thinks the boy was brave? Who thinks he was foolish? Who admires the boy's obedience to his father? Who thinks he should have shown initiative and tried to save himself? Get pupils to list arguments on each side.

→ Get the pupils to think of modern examples of courage that could be celebrated in a similar way to Hemans' poem? Whose courage would they like to honour and commemorate and why?

Perhaps because so many school children were forced to learn the poem by heart, perhaps because in part this task was, undertaken to try to inculcate into their young minds the belief in the nobility of self-sacrifice and obedience to their elders, the poem has been frequently subverted by parodists, such as this anonymous one:

> The boy stood on the burning deck,
> Picking his nose like mad.
> He was rolling it up in little balls,
> and throwing them at his dad.

→ Give pupils the first two lines of the following parodies. Their task is to complete either or both quatrains, following the ballad metre [i.e. cross-rhymed, alternating lines of four and three beats]. The 'answers' are at the bottom of the next page.

> 1. The boy stood on the burning deck
>    His lips were all a-quiver...

> 2. The boy stood on the burning deck
>    His feet were full of blisters...

Of course, the most ambitious writers might want to write an entire new stanza of their own devising such as this rather moderate one I've just knocked out:

> The boy stood on the burning deck
> Pulling a selfie smile,
> Amid the fast disappearing wreck,
> 'Me, at The Battle of the Nile'.

Here's another anonymous parody that made me laugh and which you might share with your class:

> The boy stood on the burning deck
> Playing a game of cricket
> The ball rolled up his trouser leg
> And hit his middle wicket.

1. He gave a cough, his leg fell off
And floated down the river

2. He climbed aloft, his pants fell off
And now he wears his sister's

·

# John Keats [1795-1821]

## *This Living Hand*

This living hand, now warm and capable
Of earnest grasping, would, if it were cold
And in the icy silence of the tomb,
So haunt thy days and chill thy dreaming nights
That thou would wish thine own heart dry of blood
So in my veins red life might stream again,
And thou be conscience-calm'd—see here it is—
I hold it towards you.

## The Poet

Like Byron and Shelley, both of whom he knew, John Keats was a second-generation Romantic poet who died tragically young, in his case aged just twenty-five. Before dedicating his life to poetry, Keats had trained as a doctor and had nursed a brother who died of consumption. So, when the young poet himself coughed up blood and realised from its colour that it was arterial blood, he knew he was dying. The epitaph on Keats' grave in Rome, where he was sent to enjoy the warmer climate, reads, 'Here lies one / whose name was writ on water'.

## The Poem

Really this is a fragment rather than a poem, but its fragmentary nature suits the subject well. We don't know whether it was meant to be a speech by a character in a play or not, but legend has it, that Keats scribbled it down in the margins of a manuscript moments before he died. It's a strikingly dramatic, uncanny little poem about trying to bridge the ultimate divides - between the dead and the living, between the writer and the reader, between the past and the present - so that these opposite poles can touch. The start of the poem reminds us that once these words were written and, indeed, spoken by a living, thinking, breathing human being and that his grasp of life was just as 'earnest' as anyone else's, and our own. By the second line Keats has introduced the idea of his own death and the 'icy silence of the tomb' that will silence the voice speaking to us as we read.

The addressee will be so haunted by the idea of the hand's death that they will wish to give their own blood to make it live again. The shortened, broken-off last line holds out the hand directly towards us, as if pleading for help, and makes us feel we could and should reach back through time, make contact, lend a hand.

## The Teaching Ideas

➔     This short fragment of a poem can fairly easily be learnt by heart. Hearing it spoken aloud really helps convey its powerful directness. You can a hear a terrific version as part of a short TED talk on the importance of poetry: https://www.ted.com/talks/stephen_burt_why_people_need_poetry

➜     Add a few words of your own to a poem. Start off with obvious additions - banana, snowball, ox etc. words that are clearly out of place. Once pupils are familiar with the game, make more subtle, but unnecessary additions, such as intensifiers. Before they read Keats' poem give this version to your class. See if they can spot the additions. Five points for each rogue word they identify.

> This living hand, now so warm and capable
> Of earnest grasping, would, if it were cold
> And in the icy cold silence of the tomb,
> So haunt thy living days and chill thy dreaming nights
> That thou would wish thine own very warm heart dry of blood
> So in my dead veins red life might stream again,
> And thou be so conscience-calm'd – see here it is –
> I hold it out towards you.

# William Barnes [1801 - 1886]

## *My Orcha'd in Linden Lea*

'Ithin the woodlands, flow'ry gleaded,
By the woak tree's mossy moot,
The sheenen grass-bleades, timber-sheaded,
Now do quiver under voot ;
An' birds do whissle over head,
An' water's bubblen in its bed,
An' there vor me the apple tree
Do lean down low in Linden Lea.

When leaves that leately wer a-springen
Now do feade 'ithin the copse,
An' painted birds do hush their zingen
Up upon the timber's tops;
An' brown-leav'd fruit's a turnen red,
In cloudless zunsheen, over head,
Wi' fruit vor me, the apple tree
Do lean down low in Linden Lea.

Let other vo'k meake money vaster
In the air o' dark-room'd towns,
I don't dread a peevish measter;
Though noo man do heed my frowns,
I be free to goo abrode,
Or teake agean my hwomeward road
To where, vor me, the apple tree
Do lean down low in Linden Lea.

## The Poet

Like Robert Burns, William Barnes wrote his poems in phonetically spelt dialect, in his case the dialect of his native Dorset. Variously a solicitor's clerk, a schoolmaster and a minister in the Church of England, Barnes was a prodigious linguist, fluent in Greek, Latin and several modern European languages.

## The Poem

The sonic richness of this very English lyrical poem in Romantic vein is generated by Barnes' dense packing of a limited range of similar sounds. Take, for example, the last line of the first stanza: 'Do lean down low in Linden Lea'. Firstly, and most obviously, there are two alliterative sounds that stitch the words together, the 'd' and 'l'. Added to that are two different 'ow' sounds and the four 'n's of 'lean', 'down', 'Linden'. The alternating of first consonants in the first four words, d, l, d, l works with the vowel music - 'oo', 'ee', 'ow', 'o' - to create almost a ding dong effect. In addition, Barnes thickens the iambic tetrameter by connecting the unstressed words ['do' and 'down'] through sound and giving them meaning-carrying significance. Only the preposition 'in' is really unstressed and even that word rings a little through the run of final 'n' sounds preceding it. Finally, the run of packed monosyllables, with their long rounded vowels at the start of the line allows a lightening up and opening out in the last three words, where two shorter vowels are followed by the longer, rhyming one 'in **Lind**en **Lea**' and where Linden is the first two-syllable word in the line.

Barnes believed that the English language could be purified by the removal of Latin and Greek words. Check this poem and you'll struggle to find any words from these sources. What you'll find instead is archaic-sounding verb forms, such as 'a-singen' that wouldn't might out of place in Chaucer's work, and simple changes to standard spelling that magically make words more evocative of the things they describe, such as 'sheenen' and 'bubblen'.

The sentiment in the poem is conventionally Romantic. Benign nature provides a bower for the wandering poet, a space offering deep spiritual beauty, in contrast to the material rewards of the world of work. Moreover, this bounty is free to anyone and everyone.

## The Teaching Ideas

➜     Obviously this is another poem that pupils might have fun trying to read aloud in as authentic a Dorset accent as they can manage. You can find recordings online and you might like to share the musical setting by Ralph Vaughan Williams.

➜     There are several ways in which Barnes' alters Standard English so that the words create the Dorset accent. What is the dominant accent of your region? What are some of the most common dialect words from this region? Listening carefully to their classmates and, perhaps, their teacher, talented pupils might be able to write a few lines or sentences spelt phonetically. Or perhaps the class could research writing in their local dialect before having a go at writing some. There are some entertaining 'weather maps of accents' online, including this one: https://www.youtube.com/watch?v=FyyT2jmVPAk

➜     You could demonstrate how Barnes' knits the poem's thick sonic texture, as I have tried to do above. The pupils' task would be to find other lines and identify the sonic patterns that create the poem's lush richness.

➜     What do the pupils think of the sentiment the poem expresses? Is nature still a bower for them? Do they have places they can go, sanctuaries where they can find some peace and quiet? Where are their own Linden Leas? Which sanctuary do they find more appealing, Barnes' or the one Yeats describes in *The Lake Isle of Innisfree*? [See p.146]

➜     For a different take on the attractions of escaping the world, read the wonderful, wise Italian Folktale, *The Land Where One Never Dies*, in the classic collection by Italo Calvino, available online here: http://lets-talk-story.tumblr.com/post/49418722478/the-land-where-one-never-dies

# Alfred Lord Tennyson [1809 -1892]

## *The Eagle*

He clasps the crag with crooked hands;
Close to the sun in lonely lands,
Ring'd with the azure world, he stands.

The wrinkled sea beneath him crawls;
He watches from his mountain walls,
And like a thunderbolt he falls.

# The Charge of the Light Brigade

I

Half a league, half a league,
Half a league onward,
All in the valley of Death
Rode the six hundred.
"Forward, the Light Brigade!
Charge for the guns!" he said.
Into the valley of Death
Rode the six hundred.

II

"Forward, the Light Brigade!"
Was there a man dismayed?
Not though the soldier knew
Someone had blundered.
Theirs not to make reply,
Theirs not to reason why,
Theirs but to do and die.
Into the valley of Death
Rode the six hundred.

III

Cannon to right of them,
Cannon to left of them,
Cannon in front of them
Volleyed and thundered;
Stormed at with shot and shell,
Boldly they rode and well,
Into the jaws of Death,
Into the mouth of hell
Rode the six hundred.

IV

Flashed all their sabres bare,
Flashed as they turned in air
Sabring the gunners there,
Charging an army, while
All the world wondered.
Plunged in the battery-smoke
Right through the line they broke;
Cossack and Russian
Reeled from the sabre stroke
Shattered and sundered.
Then they rode back, but not
Not the six hundred.

V

Cannon to right of them,
Cannon to left of them,
Cannon behind them
Volleyed and thundered;
Stormed at with shot and shell,
While horse and hero fell.
They that had fought so well
Came through the jaws of Death,
Back from the mouth of hell,
All that was left of them,
Left of six hundred.

VI

When can their glory fade?
O the wild charge they made!
All the world wondered.
Honour the charge they made!
Honour the Light Brigade,
Noble six hundred!

# The Poet

Still proudly holding the 'biggest beard in poetry' prize, despite being dead for over a hundred years, Alfred Lord Tennyson was the foremost poet of the Victorian age and one of the greatest English poets to ever live. Tall, gangly, short-sighted, long-haired and, of course, long-bearded, Tennyson cut an wizardy, otherworldly figure. Google photos of the lugubrious poet and you'll find a man who rarely looked directly at the camera, a man who always seemed to have something very weighty pressing on his capacious mind.

Tennyson's range was extraordinary. He was capable of writing rousing public poems, such as *The Charge of the Light Brigade*, personal poems of deep mourning, such as *In Memoriam*, narrative poems in the trendy medieval vein, poems expressing Victorian ideals of valour, as well as tender, erotic lyrics, such as the wonderful *The Crimson Petal and the White*.

# The Poems

*The Eagle* is a tensed spring of a poem. The tension is only released on the explosive word 'thunderbolt', the point at which the eagle suddenly switches from watchful stillness to a deadly action. Tennyson crams a lot of detail into two tercets and just six lines. There is the world of the majestic eagle - the crags, the mountain walls, the azure sky that all seem his, and my favourite line, 'the wrinkled sea' which 'beneath him crawls'. The adjective 'wrinkled' is an unexpected, but brilliant touch. Visually it works; waves from above could look like wrinkles, but the adjective also suggests great age and even weakness. Subtlely Tennyson takes us into the eagle's haughty perspective; the line expresses the eagle's sense of superiority, mastery - the sea is literally, but also metaphorically 'beneath' him and to him it seems to 'crawl', like frightened prey.

*The Charge of the Light Brigade* is a remarkably dynamic piece of writing. There's the noisy, filmic vividness of its depiction of battle, with cavalry charging and crashing, men and weaponry and horses shattering and sundering, smoke and the booming of cannons, the flashing of sabres and so forth. But more than the choices of dynamic verbs and colourful imagery, more than the rhetorical patterning of syntax and heavy use of repetition, it's the pummelling rhythm of the short lines that really drives this poem and makes it memorable.

The poem starts at full-tilt and thunders along until the final line. Stressed syllables are in bold:

Half a **league**, half a **league**
Half a **league** on**ward**.

DUD di **DUM**, DUD di **DUM**
DUD di **DUM**, di DUM

You may recognise this three-foot metrical foot from Pope's poem as an amphimacer. It's the dominant metre in the poem, although Tennyson sometimes lengthens the poem's stride into anapests by adding an extra unstressed syllable, so that DUD di **DUM** becomes di di **DUM**.

Anyhow, we analyse this poem in far more detail in other books in this series. Before leaving it, however, it's worth noting that 1. Tennyson had no battle experience and 2. that despite all the violence in the poem there appears to be no bloodshed, pain or suffering and 3. The depiction of doomed, self-sacrificing, obedient heroism - 'there's not to reason why / there's but to do and die' - recalls Hemans' poem and raises similar problems about blind allegiance for modern readers.

## The Teaching Ideas

→    With its shortness, tension and explosive final line that ends on the verb 'falls', *The Eagle* is a perfect poem to learn by heart and to read with an exaggerated sense of drama. Pupils could try variations in tone, pacing, volume in order to make the last line as dramatic as possible. One way to do this is to leave a short pause between the first four words in the last line, with a rising inflection and increasing volume, so that there is a crescendo on THUNDERBOLT:

And - like -     a     -     **THUNDERBOLT!** He falls

➜    Does the eagle have to be male? Does the creature described have to be an eagle? What would happen if you presented the poem to the class shorn of its title and with all the pronouns feminised? An interesting experiment would be to give half the class the male version, without the title and the other half the feminised one. Each half could write down their impressions of the central character and their ideas about what sort of a person/ creature it is. The experiment could lead into some revealing discussion of gender and representation in literature and elsewhere...

> She clasps the crag with crooked hands;
> Close to the sun in lonely lands,
> Ring'd with the azure world, she stands.
>
> The wrinkled sea beneath her crawls;
> She watches from her mountain walls,
> And like a thunderbolt she falls.

➜    Often a great poem on the page looks monumental, fixed, as if it always, inevitably must have been like that. Before introducing *The Charge of the Light Brigade* to the class try to take pupils back into the process of its composition and make them have a go at making the sorts of decisions that Tennyson had to make. [There's a great lead in to this exercise and discussion of the poem in Stephen Fry's clever and helpful book **The Ode Less Travelled**, pp.158-161.] You'll need to give the class the bare bones of the story of the catastrophe of Balaclava and their task, as a renowned

Victorian poet and Poet Laureate, of commemorating it in a suitably patriotic way. To sequence the battle, and the poem, they could produce a storyboard, perhaps. Pupils will only need a short time to sketch out a few ideas with the aim of knocking out the just the first few lines of a poem. As it's a cavalry charge, they'll need to decide what sort of rhythm they should choose and the length of the poem's lines and so forth.

➔ Once they've had enough of this task, they'll have been primed to notice Tennyson's compositional skill and, in particular, the genius of his management of metre and rhythm.

➔ While we must admire Tennyson's artistry, as I have already suggested, we might question his depiction of war and of heroism. For instance, Tennyson's poem presents war as a sort of sport, a boys' own adventure, full of dynamic action. Comparing his poem to any by Wilfred Owen will be revealing. *Dulce et Decorum Est* nearly always hits home and hard with mature Year 9 pupils.

➔ What would the aftermath of this battle have looked like? What were the scenes after the horses had reeled away and galloped off? What would happen if the battle was told from a different perspective? There's a brilliant modern re-telling by the Irish poet Ciaran Carson in the Forward anthology, *Poems of the Decade*. In stark contrast to Tennyson, Carson uses long, strung-out lines, that recall lines of troops in battle, and shifts the perspective to that of an infantryman caught up in the brutal fighting.

➔ With its pounding rhythm of galloping horses, *The Charge of the Light Brigade* also lends itself to group performances of tremendous brio. Give this poem plenty of welly.

# Edward Lear [1812-1888]

## Limericks

There was an Old Man with a beard,
Who said, "It is just as I feared!—
Two Owls and a Hen, four Larks and a Wren,
Have all built their nests in my beard.


There was an old man from Peru
who dreamed he was eating his shoe.
When he woke in a fright
in the dark of the night
he found it was perfectly true.

# The Akond of Swat

Who, or why, or which, or WHAT, Is the Akond of SWAT?

Is he tall or short, or dark or fair?
Does he sit on a stool or a sofa or chair, or SQUAT,
The Akond of Swat?

Is he wise or foolish, young or old?
Does he drink his soup and his coffee cold, or HOT,
The Akond of Swat?

Does he sing or whistle, jabber or talk,
And when riding abroad does he gallop or walk, or TROT,
The Akond of Swat?

Does he wear a turban, a fez, or a hat?
Does he sleep on a mattress, a bed, or a mat, or a COT,
The Akond of Swat?

When he writes a copy in round-hand size,
Does he cross his T's and finish his I's with a DOT,
The Akond of Swat?

Can he write a letter concisely clear
Without a speck or a smudge or smear or BLOT,
The Akond of Swat?

Do his people like him extremely well?
Or do they, whenever they can, rebel, or PLOT,
At the Akond of Swat?

If he catches them then, either old or young,
Does he have them chopped in pieces or hung, or SHOT,
The Akond of Swat?

Do his people prig in the lanes or park?
Or even at times, when days are dark, GAROTTE?
O the Akond of Swat!

Does he study the wants of his own dominion?
Or doesn't he care for public opinion a JOT,
The Akond of Swat?

To amuse his mind do his people show him
Pictures, or any one's last new poem, or WHAT,
For the Akond of Swat?

At night if he suddenly screams and wakes,
Do they bring him only a few small cakes, or a LOT,
For the Akond of Swat?

Does he live on turnips, tea, or tripe?
Does he like his shawl to be marked with a stripe, or a DOT,
The Akond of Swat?

Does he like to lie on his back in a boat
Like the lady who lived in that isle remote, SHALLOTT,
The Akond of Swat?

Is he quiet, or always making a fuss?
Is his steward a Swiss or a Swede or a Russ, or a SCOT,
The Akond of Swat?

Does he like to sit by the calm blue wave?
Or to sleep and snore in a dark green cave, or a GROTT,
The Akond of Swat?

Does he drink small beer from a silver jug?
Or a bowl? or a glass? or a cup? or a mug? or a POT,
The Akond of Swat?

Does he beat his wife with a gold-topped pipe,
When she lets the gooseberries grow too ripe, or ROT,
The Akond of Swat?

Does he wear a white tie when he dines with friends,
And tie it neat in a bow with ends, or a KNOT,
   The Akond of Swat?

Does he like new cream, and hate mince-pies?
When he looks at the sun does he wink his eyes, or NOT,
   The Akond of Swat?

Does he teach his subjects to roast and bake?
Does he sail about on an inland lake, in a YACHT,
   The Akond of Swat?

Some one, or nobody, knows I wot
Who or which or why or what
   Is the Akond of Swat!

# The Poet

The twentieth child of twenty-one children, well-travelled writer, artist and musician, Edward Lear really wanted to be a famous painter. The nonsense poetry he wrote, and which sold extremely well, was written merely for entertainment. Despite a modest background, and despite having had little formal education or training, Lear's wide-ranging talents ensured he had a highly successful career, though mainly as a writer.

# The Poems

Lear's limericks follow the same basic formula: A single, singular character is introduced, a 'young boy', 'old lady' and so forth, who has something peculiar and distinctive about them - a huge beard, penchant for eating shoes etc. - to whom something amusing happens as a result of this peculiarity. Scholars suggest that, a misfit himself, Lear may have identified with these comical creations.

In his nonsense poems Lear created fictional animals, places and characters, including this fictional type of emperor [an Akond] of the fictional land of Squat. The pleasure of the poem comes from the variations in the repeated patterns of the metre and from the variations in the refrain, so that the reader is encouraged to anticipate each end-rhyme.

# The Teaching Ideas

➜ The limerick is an undemanding, but satisfying form to write.

➜ Blanking out some of the rhyme words, and even the odd line from *The Akond of Swat* in a cloze exercise would test your pupils' capacity for rhyming. Those in need of a stiffer challenge could compose their own couplets:

Does he buy his suits in a famous shop?
Does he tie his ties with a windsor knot?
Does he wear socks? The Akond of Swat.

# Robert Browning [1812 - 1889]

## *The Laboratory*

Now that I, tying thy glass mask tightly,
May gaze thro' these faint smokes curling whitely,
As thou pliest thy trade in this devil's-smithy —
Which is the poison to poison her, prithee?

He is with her, and they know that I know
Where they are, what they do: they believe my tears flow
While they laugh, laugh at me, at me fled to the drear
Empty church, to pray God in, for them! — I am here.

Grind away, moisten and mash up thy paste,
Pound at thy powder, — I am not in haste!
Better sit thus and observe thy strange things,
Than go where men wait me and dance at the King's.

That in the mortar — you call it a gum?
Ah, the brave tree whence such gold oozings come!
And yonder soft phial, the exquisite blue,
Sure to taste sweetly, — is that poison too?

Had I but all of them, thee and thy treasures,
What a wild crowd of invisible pleasures!
To carry pure death in an earring, a casket,
A signet, a fan-mount, a filigree basket!

Soon, at the King's, a mere lozenge to give
And Pauline should have just thirty minutes to live!
But to light a pastile, and Elise, with her head
And her breast and her arms and her hands, should drop dead!

Quick — is it finished? The colour's too grim!
Why not soft like the phial's, enticing and dim?
Let it brighten her drink, let her turn it and stir,
And try it and taste, ere she fix and prefer!

What a drop! She's not little, no minion like me —
That's why she ensnared him: this never will free
The soul from those masculine eyes, — say, "no!"
To that pulse's magnificent come-and-go.

For only last night, as they whispered, I brought
My own eyes to bear on her so, that I thought
Could I keep them one half minute fixed, she would fall,
Shrivelled; she fell not; yet this does it all!

Not that I bid you spare her the pain!
Let death be felt and the proof remain;
Brand, burn up, bite into its grace —
He is sure to remember her dying face!

Is it done? Take my mask off! Nay, be not morose;
It kills her, and this prevents seeing it close:
The delicate droplet, my whole fortune's fee —
If it hurts her, beside, can it ever hurt me?

Now, take all my jewels, gorge gold to your fill,
You may kiss me, old man, on my mouth if you will!
But brush this dust off me, lest horror it brings
Ere I know it — next moment I dance at the King's!

# The Poet

Victorian poet Robert Browning is best known for his mastery of the dramatic monologue form and for his marriage to fellow poet, Elizabeth Barrett Browning. In canonical poems, such as *My Last Duchess*, *Porphyria's Lover* and, here, in *The Laboratory* the poet takes us into the minds of psychotic and murderous characters. In some of these great dramatic monologues the speaker's disturbed state of mind is hidden beneath a veil of elegant language. In *The Laboratory*, however, despite the formal control and external order, the psychosis is always bubbling away vigorously, always threatening to break out and flood the poem's surface.

Before he was himself famous, Browning fell in love with already established poet Elizabeth Barrett. But her family barred them from marrying because of Robert's lowly status and relative poverty. Undetered, the couple eloped to Italy and were duly married. Elizabeth may have been disinherited by her father and cut off from her family, but the two poets seemed to have lived a happy and fulfilling life together.

## The Poem

On the surface, the poem looks orderly. There are regular quatrains set out neatly on the page, each completing itself in its final line. Then there is the well-maintained couplet rhyme scheme. Mostly masculine in form, the rhymes are all full and click into place with machined precision. Perhaps this outer order is analogous to the outward appearance of this insanely jealous narrator. If so, only a little closer inspection of the poem would reveal her disturbed personality. We don't even have to read the words; just look at the crazy, erratic, urgent punctuation! So many question marks and exclamation marks and so many skittish dashes! Add to that the number of caesuras breaking up the pattern of the verse. Not having to read the words to work this out is analogous to not having to hear the woman speak to recognise the dark disorder of her mind.

The most shockingly disturbing lines are the ones in which she imagines the pleasure she will gain from carrying her secret, deadly power about her person, and when she speaks with such sadistic relish about the cowardly murder she hopes to perform: Referring to her rival's face she says, 'Brand, burn up, bite into its grace'. How would you describe the tone here? Bitter and twisted? Snarling and aggressive? Coolly amused? Browning positions the reader as the silent addressee of this feverish monologue, as if we are the woman's confidant or even her accomplice. Why? What effect does this have do you think?

## The Teaching Ideas

➔ Browning creates a very distinctive voice for his poisoner and leaves the story before she can do her worst. Pupils could continue the narrative, describing what happened at the dance. Their aim would be to maintain the same voice while working in a different form. To maintain the unsettling sense of intimacy between speaker and reader that makes us almost feel complicit with the potential crime, a diary form would suit this story. Or if pupils prefer to choose more straightforward narrative, you could discuss the use and function of interior monologue. An effective scene could be created, for instance, with polite, but stilted dialogue between the principal characters interspersed with the narrator's interior monologue of raging malevolence. Using the present tense would add further tension to the piece.

➔ That great show-off, the 'Bard of Avon', Shakespeare was fond of giving his villains soliloquies early in a play. Both Iago and Edmund, for instance, speak the first soliloquies in **Othello** and **King Lear** respectively, and **Richard III** opens the action in the eponymous play. A more modern example from TV of a similar device would be both the British and American versions of **House of Cards**, where the Prime Minister/ President speaks through the camera directly to the audience, as if only he is aware of our presence. Can  you or students think of any other examples? If you gave them a quick narrative summary, pupils could read and watch one of Shakespeare's villain's speeches and consider the intended effects on the audience. Are we simply appalled? Does the villain try to get us on their side? Is there a bit of us that wants to see if the villain can succeed with his nasty scheming? Surely not!

➔ There has already been a creative writing task creating a villain [see the extract from **Paradise Lost** for more details]. For this exercise pupils could either take the villain they have already created or they could imagine a new one. Following Browning's and Shakespeare's examples, they should write a couple of paragraphs in which their character speaks directly to the reader, taking us into his or her confidence about the arch villainy they will soon be carrying out. The villain could address us as an accomplice, as a friend, as somebody to confess to, or they could taunt us with our powerlessness to prevent their evil machinations...This could be a stand-alone exercise or the lead in to a longer piece of story writing.

➔ 'Female villains are scarier and more disturbing than male villains.' Discuss this proposition, sensitively, as a class.

# Emily Brontë [1818 - 1848]

## Love is Like the Wild Rose Briar

Love is like the wild rose-briar,
Friendship like the holly-tree —
The holly is dark when the rose-briar blooms
But which will bloom most constantly?

The wild rose-briar is sweet in spring,
Its summer blossoms scent the air;
Yet wait till winter comes again
And who will call the wild-briar fair?

Then scorn the silly rose-wreath now
And deck thee with the holly's sheen,
That when December blights thy brow
He still may leave thy garland green.

## The Poet

The author of the Gothic Romance **Wuthering Heights**, Emily Brontë was one of an extraordinarily creative group of siblings. Both her sisters, Charlotte and Anne, became famous novelists and her brother, Branwell, was an artist. Brought up together in a parsonage in the small town of Howarth in West Yorkshire, the Brontë children created an imaginary world, Gondal, about which they wrote stories. Relatively little is known about Emily's life. She appears, it seems, to have been a reclusive figure, shy and withdrawn, but with a great love and empathy for nature, the moors in particular, and all its creatures. Though she was sensitive, she must also have been robust and determined. Life in Howarth in the first half of the nineteenth century could be harsh, especially perhaps for sensitive young women. One way to escape was through writing and these three young women hoped to have their writing published. But to be published, the Brontë sisters had to adopt male names, with Emily becoming Ellis Bell.

## The Poem

Brontë's song-like poem begins with a familiar formula, 'love is like', setting readers up with an expectation for another celebratory poem on the wonders of being in love. The simile of love as a rose is also familiar, recalling Burns' 'Oh my love is like a red, red rose'. Characteristically for the writer of **Wuthering Heights**, Brontë's rose is 'wild' and a 'briar', which implies thorns. The second line takes the poem in an unexpected direction. We have another simile and this forms a comparison and a contrast, underlined by the repeated syntax of the first two lines and the nature imagery they share.

For then on, the poet develops this comparison, contrasting the immediate, sensual, but short-lived appeal of the rose, so 'sweet in spring', with the constant 'bloom' of friendship of the holly-tree. A neat metaphor at the end - 'December' standing in for coldness, suffering, misery - clinches the argument. Nurture it, surround yourself with it and friendship will stay with you and lift your spirits, however, low, when fickle love has gone.

# The Teaching Ideas

➜    Before reading this poem, give one half of the class the opening line 'Love is like...' and the other half 'Friendship is like...' Either they can try to think of as many metaphors as they can, or they can choose one metaphor and list as many ways this concrete thing they've chosen is like love or friendship. Of course, they don't have to write about romantic love, though they can if they like; they could write about the love between children and parents and grandparents. Gather some ideas from the class. From this list of metaphors, or one metaphor with various components, they can try to write their own friendship or love poem. Give them around ten minutes only. Return to this work after reading Brontë's poem and give the pupils another ten minutes or so. Let them take the work home to complete, and tell them they can submit it to you if they would like you to read it, but they don't have to.

Friendship is not like a bag of sweets
It's more like a bowl of breakfast porridge...

Love is like a great piece of skill
That takes the breath away...

➜    Now try to think of some concrete things that love and friendship are definitely not at all like. Love, I think, we could all agree is not much like an onion, for instance. Although, there is a well-known poem by Carol Ann Duffy that suggests otherwise...

➜    What is the value of friendship? What are the essential qualities of a great friend? Discuss as a class. Or debate the proposition: 'Having a great friend is more important than falling in love'. There are many buddy stories and stories about friendships that go awry. Pupils could write a reflective piece of prose on the importance of being a friend, or having a friend, or a story about a time a friendship went painfully wrong.

# Arthur Hugh Clough [1819 - 1861]

## Say not the Struggle Nought Availeth

Say not the Struggle nought Availeth
Say not the struggle nought availeth,
The labour and the wounds are vain,
The enemy faints not, nor faileth,
And as things have been they remain.

If hopes were dupes, fears may be liars;
It may be, in yon smoke concealed,
Your comrades chase e'en now the fliers,
And, but for you, possess the field.

For while the tired waves, vainly breaking
Seem here no painful inch to gain,
Far back through creeks and inlets making,
Comes silent, flooding in, the main.

And not by eastern windows only,
When daylight comes, comes in the light,
In front the sun climbs slow, how slowly,
But westward, look, the land is bright.

## The Poet

Educationalist, classicist and sometime dedicated assistant to Florence Nightingale, Arthur Hugh Clough was possessed of a sceptical, questioning spirit that often seems more modern than Victorian. Nevertheless, Clough was capable or writing rousing, stirring, heroic suff, as this poem exemplifies.

## The Poem

*Say not..* is a dramatic monologue written in the voice of a character, perhaps a soldier, trying to stir up some courage in his comrades when they seem most despairing. Appearances, the speaker reassures their listener, can be deceptive and though the situation may appear hopeless, this may an illusion only. The 'smoke' of battle, for instance, may hide 'the fliers' - presumably mobile cavalry - that may be about to ride to the rescue and save the day.

The metaphor in the third stanza is tremendous. Clough provides the perfect analogy for re-inforcements gathering unseen behind the frontline, and who may, at any point flood in, overwhelmingly, like the sea. And, as if that's not enough to fortify the faint-hearted and stiffen to the weariest limbs, Clough has another telling, brilliant metaphor, this time of light, that must inevitably and every day brighten even the darkest land.

Notice too, how cleverly Clough incorporates the idea of weakness converting suddenly to strength into the rhyme pattern of the verse. Each first and third line has a feminine rhyme, with a weak, unstressed final syllable, whereas the second and last rhymes are masculine and emphatically strong.

With its combination of archaic syntax and vocabulary, that opening sentence is striking too. The past tense of 'availeth' would already have sounded old-fashioned in Clough's time and the aged effect is increased by using 'nought' for nothing, as well as the positioning of the verb at the end of the line. The overall effect is to give the phrasing a timeless, almost biblical ring.

# The Teaching Ideas

→     The Victorians did seem rather fond of poems about gritty heroism, about being a true man, courage in adversity and so forth. Or, at least, Victorian male poets and the Edwardians who followed them, seem drawn to these masculine themes. See Tennyson, and a little later, Henley and Kipling for prime examples. Another example, for lack of space not included here, is Robert Browning's poem *Prospice*, which has some very fine lines, including:

For sudden the worst turns to best to the brave
The black minute's at end.

→     Ask the pupils to collect inspirational quotations. These might be ones they already know, that their family uses, or they may have to do some reasearch. One way to this would be to collect the quotations they can find around them in their immediate vicinity. Many schools have inspirational and some not-so-inspirational words, phrases and epigrams stuck up on displays.

→     Once you've a fair list of these quotations ask pupils to rank them from best to worst, least to most inspiring. They could complete this task individually on in pairs. Feedback as a whole group with the aim of agreeing a TOP TEN best quotations to stir the soul.

→     Make the pupils explain what makes the best quotations inspiring. Is it because the phrasing is memorable, such as Browning's use of juxtaposition? Or is the sentiment expressed particularly profound or wise? Or is it because the person who said or wrote these words was particularly impressive, or lived the things they said? Or something else? Or a combination of all of these.

→     Finally, if, like in the radio programme **Desert Island Discs** where guests can only save one piece of music, pupils could only keep one of these quotations from being destroyed which one would it be? Ask them to write the words of this favourite quotation out in their English exercise book and to think on them for a while, from time to time.

# Emily Dickinson [1830 - 1886]

## *Like Rain it Sounded till it Curved*

Like Rain it sounded till it curved
And then I knew 'twas Wind —
It walked as wet as any Wave
But swept as dry as sand —
When it had pushed itself away
To some remotest Plain
A coming as of Hosts was heard
It filled the Wells, it pleased the Pools
It warbled in the Road —
It pulled the spigot from the Hills
And let the Floods abroad —
It loosened acres, lifted seas
The sites of Centres stirred
Then like Elijah rode away
Upon a Wheel of Cloud.

# The Poet

Something terrible happened to the American poet in her twenties that led to her always dressing in a while dress and withdrawing entirely from the outside world to become a recluse. Some scholars suggest Dickinson withdrew from the puritan culture around her because she could not live with its values. Others argue that the poet was heartbroken by a failed relationship while some point to Dickinson saying she suffered a 'terror' at this point in her life, some sort of existential crisis that shook her faith profoundly. Unsurprisingly, given her disengagement with the outside world, few of Dickinson's poems were published in her life time. After her death, however, her sister discovered hundreds of poems hand-stitched into little books. Originally labelled as odd and eccentric, nowadays Dickinson is hailed as being one of the greatest of American poets and is a feminist icon.

# The Poem

The relentless lack of action in Dickinson's life seemed to have fine-tuned the poet's sensitivity to the natural world. In this poem she describes a wind that becomes a downpour which, in characteristically Dickinsonian style, threatens to wash the world away entirely. The poem showcases some of the poet's most famous idiosyncrasies, such as her fondness for dashes - sometimes she'd score these in vertically or even at odd angles - and her old-fashioned Capitalisation of Important Words. What, if anything, do these two devices add to the poem? In addition, again characteristically, Dickinson's puritan upbringing is reflected in her use of hymn-metre [alternating lines of tetrameter and trimeter, which is also ballad metre] and a religious idiom that elevates this short storm to almost apocalyptic, biblical scale.

# The Teaching Ideas

➜     Another short, dramatic poem, *Like Rain it Sounded til it Curved* lends itself to memorisation.

➜     Asking pupils to research poems about wind might be asking for trouble. Perhaps it'd be better just to compare Dickinson's poem with Housman's *On Wenlock Edge* or Ted Hughes' wind poem, appropriately called *Wind*. In both poems despite the onslaught of the weather the poem's structures remain solidly intact. What difference would it make if the poets had scattered their words across the page:

Like rain          it   sounded

       'Til

it                 curved

  And then I   knew        'twas

               Wind.

Etc.

➜   In classical literature, the wind often symbolises the forces of the imagination. What new light might this throw on the poems?

➜   Dickinson's choices of diction are often surprising. You could foreground this by presenting the poem as a cloze exercise:

> Like Rain it sounded till it curved
> And then I knew 'twas Wind —
> It ............ as wet as any Wave
> But swept as dry as sand —
> When it had pushed itself away
> To some remotest Plain
> A coming as of ............ was heard
> It filled the Wells, it pleased the Pools
> It .................. in the Road —
> It pulled the .............. from the Hills
> And let the Floods abroad —
> It .................... acres, lifted seas
> The sites of Centres ........................
> Then like ................ rode away
> Upon a .................. of Cloud.

# Christina Rossetti [1830 - 1894]

## *Precious Stones*

An emerald is as green as grass,
A ruby red as blood,
A sapphire shines as blue as heaven,
But a flint lies in the mud.

A diamond is a brilliant stone
To catch the world's desire,
An opal holds a rainbow light,
But a flint holds fire.

## The Poet

Born into an artistically super-talented Anglo-Italian family in which her father had translated the works of Dante and her brother Dante would become a celebrated painter and poet, Christina Rossetti became one of the foremost poets of the Victorian period and, alongside Elizabeth Barrett Browning, the greatest female poet of her time. Technically accomplished, Rossetti's verse is characaterised by mystical yearning, often a deep yearning for something that she can never have.

Rossetti was a champion of progressive causes, particularly the rights of women, not only in her art, but also in her actions. For example, during the Crimean War she volunteered to join Florence Nightingale's nurses and later volunteered at a charitable institution for the reclamation of 'fallen women', i.e. women who had children outside of marriage.

## The Poem

It's a clever, neat little poem with a witty reversal, like a punch line, in the final line. The use of conventional similes in the first stanza hints at the conventional perspective that would see these beautiful jewels as more valuable than the ordinary, dull-looking, disregarded flint. But the flint has something within it, a capacity for 'fire' which can be read literally as being useful, or in a more metaphorical sense. If you've been reading the rest of this book, by now you'll quickly have recognised the bouncy ballad or hymn metre. Notice how Rossetti tightens the metre in the last line, so that the poem finishes with three emphatic stresses on suitably plain monosyllables.

## The Teaching Ideas

➜    This is another poem that would lend itself to a cloze exercise. As well as blanking out a few words, I'd dock the last clinching line, so that when this is revealed pupils appreciate its cleverness a little more. Hopefully.

> An emerald is as green as .............,
> A ruby red as blood,
> A ................. shines as blue as heaven,
> But a flint lies in the ....................
>
> A diamond is a brilliant stone
> To ............. the world's desire,
> An opal holds a rainbow light,
> ......................................................

➜    Challenge pupils to think of as many different metaphors as they can to convey the same idea of hidden worth and perhaps beauty. Give them around five teacher minutes. For example, they could think of the animal world.

➜    Once they've thought of their metaphor they could have a go at writing a poem following Rossetti's example. For instance, 'The lion is a mighty beast, the hippo's big as a house, an owl is a wise old bird, but a small thing is a mouse' etc. Obviously the really tricky bit will be getting that last line right. Perhaps some bright creative spark could finish my effort off for me and send it to me...

# Lewis Carroll [1832 - 1898]

## *Jabberwocky*

'Twas brillig, and the slithy toves
Did gyre and gimble in the wabe:
All mimsy were the borogoves,
And the mome raths outgrabe.

"Beware the Jabberwock, my son!
The jaws that bite, the claws that catch!
Beware the Jubjub bird, and shun
The frumious Bandersnatch!"

He took his vorpal sword in hand;
Long time the manxome foe he sought—
So rested he by the Tumtum tree
And stood awhile in thought.

And, as in uffish thought he stood,
The Jabberwock, with eyes of flame,
Came whiffling through the tulgey wood,
And burbled as it came!

One, two! One, two! And through and through
The vorpal blade went snicker-snack!
He left it dead, and with its head
He went galumphing back.

"And hast thou slain the Jabberwock?
Come to my arms, my beamish boy!
O frabjous day! Callooh! Callay!"
He chortled in his joy.

'Twas brillig, and the slithy toves
Did gyre and gimble in the wabe:
All mimsy were the borogoves,
And the mome raths outgrabe.

## The Poet

Lewis Carroll was the pen name of Oxford mathematics don and photographer, Charles Dodgson. Carroll is most celebrated as a writer for his Alice novels, **Alice in Wonderland** and **Through the Looking Glass** and for his inventive nonsense verse.

## The Poem

The poet and critic Glynn Maxwell has suggested that poems have four major aspects and that some poems have one or other of these aspects dominant over the others. Maxwell's four aspects are solar, lunar, musical and visual. By 'solar' he means that are immediately striking, whereas 'lunar' poems are more mysterious and haunting. The ultimate visual poem would be a concrete poem and the musical counterpart would be a poem that relies entirely on sound, such as Edwin Morgan's marvellous *The Lock Ness Monster's Song* and this famous example, *Jabberwocky*.

Somehow Carroll manages to create a creepy if comical, slightly gothic atmospshere in the first [and last] stanza, despite employing lots of made-up words. Other made-up words or words used in an unfamiliar context include, 'frumious', 'maxome', 'tulgey', 'vorpal', 'whiffling', 'uffish', 'burbled', 'frabjous'. In other ways, the poem's quite conventional, telling a familiar narrative of a brave hero defeating a terrible monster, an act celebrated on his victorious return home.

## The Teaching Ideas

→   Clearly this is a poem that demands to be learn-by-heart and to be practised reciting in an OTT ham-actorly style to bring out the full dramatic effect. You can listen to Benedict Cumberbatch giving it a good old go here: www.youtube.com/watch?v=Q_Um3787fSY

→   Pupils often enjoy guessing and then comparing what all the made-up words mean. What, for example, is a 'tove'? A great challenge would be to make up some of their own that could be slotted into the poem. A fun game could be played in which pupils read out their neologisms and the rest of the class have to guess the meaning.

Taking this a step further, pupils could either try to write a new stanza that could be fitted seamlessly into Carroll's poem or make up their own nonsense poem using the same rhythm:

'Twas nickly and the nagrous sprags
were spindeling in the mire
All flatlish were the grumbeldy mites
With spines of rimelly fire.

etc. only better.

➜    Many pupils will also enjoy the chance to illustrate this poem, either as a storyboard or in terms of a portrait of the jabberwock and/ or its vanquisher. The youngest might even enjoy colouring in Tenniel's famous illustration. The more lurid the colours the better.

# Thomas Hardy [1840 - 1928]

## *The Voice*

Woman much missed, how you call to me, call to me,
Saying that now you are not as you were
When you had changed from the one who was all to me,
But as at first, when our day was fair.

Can it be you that I hear? Let me view you, then,
Standing as when I drew near to the town
Where you would wait for me: yes, as I knew you then,
Even to the original air-blue gown!

Or is it only the breeze, in its listlessness
Travelling across the wet mead to me here,
You being ever dissolved to wan wistlessness,
Heard no more again far or near?

Thus I; faltering forward,
Leaves around me falling,
Wind oozing thin through the thorn from norward,
And the woman calling.

## The Poet

Thomas Hardy is, of course, most famous for writing canonical novels including **Far From the Madding Crowd** [1874], **Tess of the D'Urbervilles** [1891] and **Jude the Obscure** [1895]. Hardy's novels often tackled controversial themes in Victorian culture, such as the position of women in society, industrialisation of agriculture and class prejudice, and Hardy supposedly abandoned novel writing after the hostile reception of the public to Jude. The novel's loss was poetry's gain.

As a poet who often used traditional forms and wrote in an unfussy, unpretentious, elegiac style, Hardy has been an important model for many English poets. His influence can be traced in the twentieth century through admirers such as Philip Larkin and Andrew Motion.

## The Poem

This is a melancholy, haunting poem about the poet being haunted by the ghost of his dead wife, whose presence he can so nearly sense as he walks alone, uncertainly, 'faltering forward' through a suitably lonely, lifeless landscape. The fact that the poem is addressed to the dead woman as if she can hear him, and as if the poet too is calling, just as he thinks he can hear her voice in the wind, makes the poem poignant. The emotional effect is increased significantly by Hardy's conversational style which implies an intimacy, a closeness between speaker and listener despite the unbridgeable gulf seperating the living from the dead: 'Can it be you that I hear?'; 'yes, as I knew you then'.

## The Teaching Ideas

➜    Deciding on narrative perspective is always a key aspect of writing a decent story. To emphasise this point and to bring out the intimacy of the poem present it first with all the pronouns changed into the third person and the verbs switched to the past tense:

> Woman much missed, how she called to him, called to him,
> Saying that now she is not as you was
> When she had changed from the one who was all to him,
> But as at first, when their day was fair.    etc.

Anaylse and discuss this altered version of the poem as if it were the real one, bringing out the isolation of the speaker, the closeness of the ghost, the importance of sounds, the use of pathetic fallacy and so forth.

➜     Then show the class Hardy's poem as he wrote it. Ask pupils to write a paragraph or two on the effect of the changes in tense and narrative perspective had on their reading of the poem.

# W. E. Henley [1849-1903]

## *Invictus*

Out of the night that covers me,
Black as the pit from pole to pole,
I thank whatever gods may be
For my unconquerable soul.

In the fell clutch of circumstance
I have not winced nor cried aloud.
Under the bludgeonings of chance
My head is bloody, but unbowed.

Beyond this place of wrath and tears
Looms but the Horror of the shade,
And yet the menace of the years
Finds and shall find me unafraid.

It matters not how strait the gate,
How charged with punishments the scroll,
I am the master of my fate,
I am the captain of my soul.

## The Poet

Late Victorian poet, editor and literary critic, W. E. Henley had to have half a leg amputated while he was still a child, an experience that may have helped to shape in him admiration for the sort of courage and fortitude expressed in his famous poem, *Invictus*, which means 'invincible' in Latin.

## The Poem

Henley's was, of course, the favourite poem of Nelson Mandela who regularly recited it for inspiration during his twenty-seven years of incarceration in Robben Island prison. As the actor Morgan Freeman, who played Mandela in the 2009 film named after the poem, **Invictus**, says, the 'poem was his favourite… When he lost courage, when he felt like just giving up — just lie down and not get up again — he would recite it. And it would give him what he needed to keep going.'

It starts with complete universal darkness, a night that completely 'covers' both the speaker and, in a powerful piece of hyperbole, the whole of the globe, 'from pole to pole'. Ominously, the darkness is 'black as the pit', with connotations of hell, an image echoed in the later phrase 'Horror of the shade'. Henley expresses a Late Victorian sceptical mentality; he does not thank the Christian God for his strength, but 'whatever gods may be'. In the final lines he goes, further, declaring in stirringly defiant, humanist terms that he is the 'captain' of his soul.

## The Teaching Ideas

It's the great phrasing that makes *Invictus* such a powerful, memorable poem. The sense of challenges faced down, of suffering, fear, pain and punishment born with courage are made palpable and make the stoical defiance the more admirable.

→   A cloze exercise would help highlight Henley's excellent choices of words to create vivid concrete images.

Out of the night that covers me,
Black as the ............. from pole to pole,
I thank whatever gods may be
For my ............. soul.

In the fell ................ of circumstance
I have not winced nor cried aloud.
Under the ................... of chance
My head is bloody, but ....................

Beyond this place of wrath and tears
Looms but the ............. of the shade,
And yet the menace of the years
Finds and shall find me ....................

It matters not how strait the gate,
How charged with punishments the scroll,
I am the master of my fate,
I am the ...................... of my soul.

➔    A number of the poems in this anthology explore or express the nature of heroism/ courage/ manliness. *The Charge of the Light Brigade*, *Jabberwocky* and *If* spring immediately to mind, all of which, interestingly enough, are Victorian poems. From examining these poems what appear to be the most important qualities to a manly Victorian hero? How might this be different from a modern hero, or a real-life hero, like Nelson Mandela?

➔    What different kinds of heroes are there? Or put another way, what are the range of qualities heroes can have? How, for instance, is Sherlock Holmes a different type of hero to James Bond and how is James Bond different to Batman? Or, indeed, how is the modern James Bond different from his 1960's incarnation? As with the exercise on literary villains, prompted by the extract from **Paradise Lost**, pupils could be challenged to list as many literary/ film heroes as they can in 5-10 minutes.

➜ Developing this work further, pupils could make up a new hero and describe them in a couple of paragraphs as the heor goes about doing characteristically heroic things. If they created a monster or villain in work based on earlier poems in the anthology they'd now have two characters destined to collide in an explosive story...

➜ An alternative, less narrative driven exercise, would be to write a couple of paragraphs or so on any real people the pupils consider to be true heroes. Famous people like Nelson Mandela, Tanni Grey-Thompson, Winston Churchill, or members of their family, perhaps, or people who quietly go about doing heroic work, such as nurses and teachers, and English teachers in particular, of course.

# Anonymous

## *Donal Og* (translated from Irish by Lady Augusta Gregory [1852 - 1932])

It is late last night the dog was speaking of you;
the snipe was speaking of you in her deep marsh.
It is you are the lonely bird through the woods;
and that you may be without a mate until you find me.

You promised me, and you said a lie to me,
that you would be before me where the sheep are flocked;
I gave a whistle and three hundred cries to you,
and I found nothing there but a bleating lamb.

You promised me a thing that was hard for you,
a ship of gold under a silver mast;
twelve towns with a market in all of them,
and a fine white court by the side of the sea.

You promised me a thing that is not possible,
that you would give me gloves of the skin of a fish;
that you would give me shoes of the skin of a bird;
and a suit of the dearest silk in Ireland.

When I go by myself to the Well of Loneliness,
I sit down and I go through my trouble;
when I see the world and do not see my boy,
he that has an amber shade in his hair.

It was on that Sunday I gave my love to you;
the Sunday that is last before Easter Sunday
and myself on my knees reading the Passion;
and my two eyes giving love to you for ever.

My mother has said to me not to be talking with you today,
or tomorrow, or on the Sunday;

it was a bad time she took for telling me that;
it was shutting the door after the house was robbed.

My heart is as black as the blackness of the sloe,
or as the black coal that is on the smith's forge;
or as the sole of a shoe left in white halls;
it was you put that darkness over my life.

You have taken the east from me, you have taken the west from
me;
you have taken what is before me and what is behind me;
you have taken the moon, you have taken the sun from me;
and my fear is great that you have taken God from me!

# The Poet

Anonymous is a pretty prolific writer of poetry. This rather good one was translated by Lady Augusta Gregory, friend and patron of W. B. Yeats, among others. Like Yeats, Lady Gregory was fascinated by folklore and by the theatre and the two friends must have had many interesting conversations while Yeats stayed at Gregory's ancestral home of Coole Park in Galway. With Yeats, Gregory was a supporter of the Irish Literary Revival and of the Abbey theatre which staged several of her plays.

# The Poem

It's a beautiful, powerful lament, is it not? A dramatic monologue in the impassioned voice of a woman betrayed in love, knowing that her credulity and her love have been exploited, but, agonisingly, still so in love with the man she knows 'lied' to her and offered her beautiful, but impossible things. Still a young woman, whose mother prohibited the relationship far too late in the day, at the end of the poem she feels bereft, as if her life is empty, directionless, finished.

There are so many great images and memorable lines; the ship 'of gold under a silver mast'; the gloves 'of the skin of a fish'; the heart 'black as the blackness of a sloe'. The there's the sense of desolation that builds through the obsessive reframing of her sense of loss in the last stanza, whose opening lines about the 'east and 'west' may have prompted similar ones in W. H. Auden's lament *Stop All the Clocks*.

# The Teaching Ideas

➔    Pupils should select five things they like best about the poem. These could be images, specific words, lines, the rhythm, use of repetition anything specific they can pull out, quote and inspect more closely. Once they've made their own selection they could compare with a partner or with a small group. Did everyone pick the same things? Through whole class discussion try to reach some sort of consensus about the best aspects of this poem. You might also discuss how we could try to define 'best' in a work of art. If you need more than five things/ quotations, that's okay, but keeping a tight limit will help pupils compare the merit of different aspects. After the discussion, they should be ready to write a few sentences on each aspect/ quotation they've chosen.

→   It's tempting to read this poem as a reply to Marlowe's and Yeats' seduction poems, both, or course, written from male perspectives. Marlowe's passionate shepherd offers similar gifts and promises, and the lyricism of *Donal Og* echoes Yeats' in *He Wishes for the Cloths of Heaven*. How might the poems have been different if *Donal Og* was written by a man and the other two written by women? Discussing this could lead to an interesting comparative essay for pupils at the end of KS3.

→   Crunching a poem entails reducing each line to what you consider to be the most important word. Working at first on their own, pupils should crunch each line of *Donal Og*. Next, they compare their crunchings with a partner. Next, their aim is to arrive at a consensus crunch between them. Feedbacking as a whole class should lead to a whole class mega-crunch of the poem. If pupils had to provide the crunchiest crunch, which five words would they say were the most inportant in the poem. Why?

A.E.Houseman [1859 - 1936]

## On Wenlock Edge

On Wenlock Edge the wood's in trouble;
His forest fleece the Wrekin heaves;
The gale, it plies the saplings double,
And thick on Severn snow the leaves.

'Twould blow like this through holt and hanger
When Uricon the city stood:
'Tis the old wind in the old anger,
But then it threshed another wood.

Then, 'twas before my time, the Roman
At yonder heaving hill would stare:
The blood that warms an English yeoman,
The thoughts that hurt him, they were there.

There, like the wind through woods in riot,
Through him the gale of life blew high;
The tree of man was never quiet:
Then 'twas the Roman, now 'tis I.

The gale, it plies the saplings double,
It blows so hard, 'twill soon be gone:
To-day the Roman and his trouble
Are ashes under Uricon.

# The Poet

A. E. Housman was a classical scholar who became Professor of Latin, first at UCL and later at Cambridge university, who only published two collections of poems during his lifetime. Characteristically Housman's poems strike an elegiac note, with a pervasive sense that time is always running out and that youthful or pastoral beauty will all too soon be gone.

# The Poem

Housman's shaping of language into metre, rhythm and rhyme seems effortless and recalls Keats' dictum that 'If Poetry comes not as naturally as Leaves to a tree it had better not come at all'. The unforced, graceful, natural effect is generated by a combination of key aspects: The unpretentious diction, the cross-rhyme pattern, the sonically-pleasing full rhymes that alternate between unstressed feminine endings, such as 'trouble' / 'double' and masculine 'heaves' / 'leaves' and the way the words run along the verse's even iambic tetrameter with each orderly quatrain completing its sentence with its final word.

The stand-out metaphor is the 'tree of man', which Housman tells us 'was never quiet'. Indeed, the poet and classical scholar gives his own life a historical perspective, presenting himself as standing in a line of previous onlookers, the Roman and the English yeoman, who have witnessed similar storms and dealt with their own troubles. 'The gale of life' might have blown through each of them 'in riot', but Housman demonstrates his ability to control and shape such potentially destructive forces and turn them into consummate art.

# The Teaching Ideas

➔ This is another poem that can be learnt by heart and recited with pleasure.

➔ It would also lend itself well to a sequencing exercise as there are enough clues to enable clever readers to work out how the poem is connected together. You could give pupils the choice of a moderate or a difficult option. For the former, just mix the order of the stanzas up; for the latter leave the first two and last two lines in the right places and then scramble all the other lines together, as if blown about by the angry old wind.

➔    As mentioned in the piece on Emily Dickinson's weather poem an interesting comparison could be made between her poem and Housman's and / or Ted Hughes' poem *Wind*.

## Rudyard Kipling [1865 - 1936]

### If

If you can keep your head when all about you
Are losing theirs and blaming it on you,
If you can trust yourself when all men doubt you,
But make allowance for their doubting too;
If you can wait and not be tired by waiting,
Or being lied about, don't deal in lies,
Or being hated, don't give way to hating,
And yet don't look too good, nor talk too wise:

If you can dream—and not make dreams your master;
If you can think—and not make thoughts your aim;
If you can meet with Triumph and Disaster
And treat those two impostors just the same;
If you can bear to hear the truth you've spoken
Twisted by knaves to make a trap for fools,

Or watch the things you gave your life to, broken,
And stoop and build 'em up with worn-out tools:

If you can make one heap of all your winnings
    And risk it on one turn of pitch-and-toss,
And lose, and start again at your beginnings
    And never breathe a word about your loss;
If you can force your heart and nerve and sinew
    To serve your turn long after they are gone,
And so hold on when there is nothing in you
    Except the Will which says to them: 'Hold on!'

If you can talk with crowds and keep your virtue,
    Or walk with Kings—nor lose the common touch,
If neither foes nor loving friends can hurt you,
    If all men count with you, but none too much;
        If you can fill the unforgiving minute
        With sixty seconds' worth of distance run,
Yours is the Earth and everything that's in it,
    And—which is more—you'll be a Man, my son!

# The Poet

Journalist, short story writer and novelist probably best known for **The Jungle Book**, Rudyard Kipling 1865-1936 has been called the 'Bard of Empire' and 'The Prophet of British Imperialism'. Though Kipling's narrative skills and technical virtuosity, especially his tremendous dexterity with metre and rhyme, are almost universally admired, his political views, particularly those concerning race, nationality and Empire, have proved problematic for many modern readers. Kipling idolised the British Empire and we don't have to be post-colonial critics to take a rather different, more nuanced perspective to the poet's.

# The Poem

Even in his own time, Kipling complained that his most famous poem, *If*, had been 'anthologised to weariness'. Nevertheless, to this day it continues to appear at the top of readers' polls of favourite poems in English and contains some of the most quoted lines of verse in the language. Perhaps Kipling's poem was, and remains, popular with a general readership because it is memorably-phrased but also understandable on a first reading. Famously, *If* outlines a description of an ideal man, according to the tastes and values of the late Victorian/ early Edwardian period. Addressed to the poet's son, the poem is a kind of instruction kit on how to assemble oneself into the heroic figure that is a true man. All you have to do, the poet advises the boy, is to develop the following list of admirable qualities, and, hey presto, you'll 'be a man, my son'.

Reading Kipling's poetry from a modern perspective, it seems clear that although it may feature plucky chaps doing brave things and although it may express sympathy for working class characters, such as the British tommy, it is very much a product of its period and of a distinctly upper-middle class, distinctly male, proudly English sensibility.

# The Teaching Ideas

➔     *If* will lend itself well to group performance, as it reads as if it should be spoken aloud, with gusto, to an audience.

➜ Focusing on the presentation of masculinity, before reading pupils could compile their own lists of an ideal man. If this is too personal, they could compile a list of masculine qualities they think our culture promotes. To help do this they could list examples of famous, celebrated men in our culture, such as sportsmen like David Beckham and Usain Bolt and musicians such as Ed Sheeran and Stormzy. Pupils should then list all the qualities Kipling valorises in *If* before making a comparison between the two. Which aspects of masculinity are still admired? How might we criticise the version of masculinity Kipling celebrates?

➜ We don't have to be hard-line feminists or post-colonialist critics to object to the grand sentiments in the final lines of the poem. If the world 'and everything that's in it' stands ready to be possessed by white English men, what's left for non-white, non-English, non-male people? Parody can be a powerful way of interacting with and contesting a text. What would Kipling's poem advising his daughter on how to be the perfect woman have been like? Potentially a little research on Victorian ideas of femininity would be useful here, starting with the ideal of the 'Angel in the House'.

'If you can sit prettily and play the piano
And not talk too loud to interrupt the men.
If you can learn to say yes and when to say no
And to embroider pretty lace around a hem'

etc. Only better.

# William Butler Yeats [1865-1939]

## *The Lake Isle of Innisfree*

I will arise and go now, and go to Innisfree,
And a small cabin build there, of clay and wattles made;
Nine bean-rows will I have there, a hive for the honey-bee,
And live alone in the bee-loud glade.

And I shall have some peace there, for peace comes dropping
slow,
Dropping from the veils of the morning to where the cricket
sings;
There midnight's all a glimmer, and noon a purple glow,
And evening full of the linnet's wings.

I will arise and go now, for always night and day
I hear lake water lapping with low sounds by the shore;
While I stand on the roadway, or on the pavements grey,
I hear it in the deep heart's core.

## He Wishes for the Cloths of Heaven

HAD I the heavens' embroidered cloths,
Enwrought with golden and silver light,
The blue and the dim and the dark cloths
Of night and light and the half-light,
I would spread the cloths under your feet:
But I, being poor, have only my dreams;
I have spread my dreams under your feet;
Tread softly because you tread on my dreams.

## The Poet

If W. B. Yeats had ever appeared on the TV programme **Escape to the Country** he would have been able to tell the presenters exactly what sort of escape he was looking for, even down to the number of rows of beans he required. It's telling, however, that when this bardic poet tried to take a sweetheart to the actual island of Innisfree he has unable to locate it! The key thing Yeats would have told the presenters is that he wanted to get away, escape from the busy modern world and return to a simpler, self-sustaining life, surrounded by natural beauty.

Dreamy, lyrical and frequently lovelorn, early Yeats poems are full of yearning for what the poet cannot quite have or cannot quite reach, most commonly love in one form or another, and more specifically his greatest love, Maud Gonne, in one form or another. The poems of Yeats' middle period shift focus from the troubles of the heart to the troubles of his country. But still, in the turbulent first decades of the twentieth century, the desire to sail away from it all is as potent as ever. Leaner and starker, Yeats' late poems grow more philosophical, circling questions of aging, morality and mortality and once again the idea of finding some sort of sanctuary from the growing darkness continues to exert a powerful tug on the aging poet's imagination. A dramatist as well as a poet, fascinated the idea of speaking from masks, a lifelong dabbler in magic and the occult, there is always something theatrical and magical about Yeats and his poetry.

## The Poems

*The Lake Isle of Innisfree* was first published in Yeats' 1893 collection, **The Rose**. It's a poem full of longing, here for a place of sanctuary rather than for a lover, as in the second of these poems. Typically in Yeats' poems the speaker hasn't yet arrived at his desires; as we join the poem he's about to 'arise and go' there, any minute now, just you watch him go. But at the start of the third stanza he uses exactly the same phrase, 'I will arise and go now', suggesting that he hasn't actually moved on in any significant sense.

Notice how the close repetition of words, such as 'go now and go to' or 'peace there, for peace' and 'dropping down/ dropping from' create a concentrated sonorous, chant-like rhythm. The poet is casting a spell on his readers, but also entrancing himself.

What he wants seems simple enough: Just a small cabin and a few comforts, bean-rows and hives that will help to sustain him. He also desires splendid isolation, to 'live alone' and to be at peace within nature. Characteristically Yeats focuses on lovely light from the sky - midnight will be 'all a glimmer, and noon a purple glow' and this rich light is complemented by tranquil near-silence, just the hum of bees and the 'lake water lapping'. That he so intently desires such 'peace' signals troubles in his life, perhaps from political or more personal sources. His rich, but simple Eden is in stark contrast with the modern world of cities, with their roadways and 'pavements grey' and it calls to the innermost emotional self of the poet, his 'deep heart's core'.

*He Wishes for the Cloths of Heaven* comes from Yeats' 1899 collection, **The Wind Among the Reeds**. It's a short, lovelorn lyric in which the poet contrasts his material poverty with his rich and generous poetic soul. It's another poem about what the poet yearns for - he doesn't have his beloved and so needs to win her heart, and he doesn't have cash to lavish on her. He does have, however, his sensitive soul and his way with words.

Typically Yeats expresses a hypothetical: 'Had he' then 'he would'. But he doesn't and so, sadly, he can't. He *would* leave the entrancing lights of the heavens at his beloved's feet, treating her like a Goddess, if he *could*, but he can't. He can, however, offer her, instead, his 'dreams'.

Complementing the visual imagery, repetition is again very pronounced. Look, for instance, at the unusual end rhymes - cloth and cloth, light and light, feet and feet. These end rhymes are perfect, exact matches, perhaps like the two lovers. Coupled with the four-beat, tetrameter, lines, the sonic close repetitive patterning generates an incantatory rhythm within which the words vibrate and resonate.

## The Teaching ideas

Do you think Yeats ever got to Innisfree, or somewhere like it? Did he even ever intend to get there? What might have been the negatives sides of his

Edenic vision? The dream of a simpler life, lived closer to nature appeals to many of us, from time to time. But is it realistic?

→   Ask pupils to discuss their idea of a perfect place to live or their idea of paradise. Would this place include modern technology? Would it have wi-fi connectivity? When would they must like to escape to it? What would they most like to escape from? If the class are hooked, the discussion could turn into a piece of extended writing, in prose or poetic form.

→   With their concetrated music, Yeats' poems can be learnt by heart fairly easily and performed either individually or in small groups. You can hear him reading *The Lake Isle of Innisfree* in his trembly vibrato, dramatic style here: www.youtube.com/watch?v=QLlcvQg9i6c.Pupils could have fun imitating this theatrical style of delivery and in finding their own style.

→   Ask pupils how they might feel if *He Wishes for the Cloths of Heaven* had been written to and for them. Would they be flattered, won over or unimpressed? Why? Their task is to write a response addressed to Yeats, either as a letter or in poetic form. For example:

If you'd  taken the heaven's embroidered cloths
With all those lovely, beautiful lights
And you'd stuck them under my feet
And asked me, nicely, to tread on them, softly,
Because the cloths of heaven were actually your dreams,
Welll, let me tell you W.B. ...

**NB**
*Donal Og* was translated by Yeats' friend and patron, Augusta Gregory. In what ways could it be read as a response to love poems such as Yeats'?

# Hilaire Belloc [1870 - 1953]

## *Tarantella*

Do you remember an Inn,
Miranda?
Do you remember an Inn?
And the tedding and the spreading
Of the straw for a bedding,
And the fleas that tease in the High Pyrenees,
And the wine that tasted of tar?
And the cheers and the jeers of the young muleteers
(Under the vine of the dark verandah)?
Do you remember an Inn, Miranda,
Do you remember an Inn?
And the cheers and the jeers of the young muleteeers
Who hadn't got a penny,
And who weren't paying any,
And the hammer at the doors and the Din?
And the Hip! Hop! Hap!
Of the clap
Of the hands to the twirl and the swirl
Of the girl gone chancing,
Glancing,
Dancing,
Backing and advancing,
Snapping of a clapper to the spin
Out and in --
And the Ting, Tong, Tang, of the Guitar.

Do you remember an Inn,
Miranda?
Do you remember an Inn?
Never more;
Miranda,
Never more.

Only the high peaks hoar:
And Aragon a torrent at the door.
No sound
In the walls of the Halls where falls
The tread
Of the feet of the dead to the ground
No sound:
But the boom
Of the far Waterfall like Doom.

## The Poet

Alongside H. G. Wells, George Bernard Shaw and G. K. Chesterton, Anglo-French poet Hilaire Belloc is considered to be one of the Big Four writers of Edwardian Letters. Built like a tank, with a vigorous disposition and fine intellect, Belloc packed a lot into his life. A prolific writer, he was also at various times a journalist, a soldier, a Liberal MP and political reformer, a historian and a sailor good enough to make the French sailing team. As a poet he is especially admired for his light verse and his poetry for children, including the unforgettable tale of that dreadful fibber *Matilda*.

## The Poem

Belloc is often classed with Lewis Carroll as a particularly talented writer of light verse. Like Carroll's *Jabberwocky*, the main pleasure of this poem is the sound of the verse. The intensely musical quality is generated by virtuosic and dynamic variations of an anapestic tetrameter, combined with an internal and triple rhyme pattern. Working together, these devices deliver lines such as, 'And the **tedd**ing and the **spread**ing / Of the **straw** for a **bedd**ing' [stressed beats in in bold; rhymes underlined.]

A poem about a fast, whirling form of dance, it is accordingly full of energetic movement and noisy sound imagery. We hear, for instance, 'cheers and jeers', hammering, the sounds of clapping and snapping, the 'ting, tong, tang' of a guitar and a final ominous 'boom'.

## The Teaching Ideas

➔   This is definitely another poem that demands to be heard and would be ideal for group performance, with pupils concentrating on bringing out the driving rhythm and its protean transitions. The story and the sense don't really matter much, these are words becoming as close to music as words can.

➔   Perhaps highly talented pupils will be able to write an extra few lines for the poem, lines which could be added smoothly into the flow of the rhythm, adding to the poem's musical dance of words.

# Walter De La Mare [1873 - 1956]

## *The Listeners*

'Is there anybody there?' said the Traveller,
Knocking on the moonlit door;
And his horse in the silence champed the grasses
Of the forest's ferny floor:
And a bird flew up out of the turret,
Above the Traveller's head:
And he smote upon the door again a second time;
'Is there anybody there?' he said.
But no one descended to the Traveller;
No head from the leaf-fringed sill
Leaned over and looked into his grey eyes,
Where he stood perplexed and still.
But only a host of phantom listeners
That dwelt in the lone house then
Stood listening in the quiet of the moonlight
To that voice from the world of men:

Stood thronging the faint moonbeams on the dark
stair,
That goes down to the empty hall,
Hearkening in an air stirred and shaken
By the lonely Traveller's call.
And he felt in his heart their strangeness,
Their stillness answering his cry,
While his horse moved, cropping the dark turf,
'Neath the starred and leafy sky;
For he suddenly smote on the door, even
Louder, and lifted his head:—
'Tell them I came, and no one answered,
That I kept my word,' he said.
Never the least stir made the listeners,
Though every word he spake
Fell echoing through the shadowiness of the still house
From the one man left awake:
Ay, they heard his foot upon the stirrup,
And the sound of iron on stone,
And how the silence surged softly backward,
When the plunging hoofs were gone.

## The Poet

Poet, novelist and short story writer, Walter De La Mare was fond of writing ghost stories and tales of imagination, among which *Seaton's Aunt*, *The Riddle* and *All Hallows* are often considered the finest. De La Mare believed children's imaginations have a visionary power, a power that can be squeezed out of us in adulthood, and he tried in his writing to express that power.

## The Poem

Moonlight. Silence. Loneliness. An empty house. A mysterious visitor. The classic ingredients for a ghost story. De La Mare's spooky, atmospheric poem raises many questions, but offers few answers. Who, or what, are these phantom listeners? Something is certainly there, inside the house; they 'dwelt in the lone house', 'stood listening' and throng to the sound of the man's voice. Ans who is this man, this traveller? Why has he come to this remote house? What message did he have? Who are the 'them' he refers to?

De La Mare employs omniscient narration adroitly, so that the perspective switches from outside to inside the house, from the traveller and his thoughts, to the listeners, and back again. There's a cinematic quality and an uncanny effect, whereby the poet, by saying that something doesn't happen, makes us imagine it did: 'No head.../ Leaned over and looked into his grey eyes'. A great last line, 'the silence surged softly backward' both personifies the absence of sound and uses slithering sibilance to make us hear silence.

## The Teaching Ideas

➔ This is another fun poem to read aloud, perhaps in groups of three, with one reader playing the traveller, another reading the narrator's lines and the third pupil reading lines that are about the listeners. The readings, should, of course, aim to be spine-chilling. Taking this a little further, pupils could rmake crackly, radio-style readings, adding suitable sound effects and music, or even produce a film poem. For inspiration, for older pupils, you could watch and listen to the haunting short film of Liz Berry's poem *The Black Delph Bride*: https://www.youtube.com/watch?v=JT0izGJCHO8

➔ Reading *The Listeners* gives us the perfect excuse for discussing and writing ghost stories. And who doesn't love a great ghost story? How is a ghost story distinct from a horror story? What are the vital ingredients? One is a creepy setting. A useful way into a ghost story is to source photos of spooky houses on the internet and give these out as visual stimuli for the stories.

Next pupils need to think of a character and why he or she is visiting this obviously haunted place. A short time frame is also useful - no more than 24 hours and pupils should aim to describe just one major event/ incident. In my experience, teachers have to steer pupils away from going into too much action and especially from splattering the story with liberal amounts of blood-and-guts. The focus of the excercise should be creating a creepy, mysterious, suspenseful atmosphere, and maintaining it - not a lot needs to actually happen, but the reader should feel that something dreadful is around each corner and is always about to take place.

Pupils should try not to give too much away about their supernatural character and perhaps no contact should actually be made. Following De La Mare's example, they should also include a least one switch in perspective from the human protagonist to whatever it is lurking in the house, watching them, licking its parched lips.

➔ To help get pupils in a spooky frame of mind you could show a carefully selected clip from the film **The Woman in Black**.

# Robert Service [1874 - 1958]

## Extracts from The Shooting of Dan McGrew

A bunch of the boys were whooping it up in the Malamute saloon;
The kid that handles the music-box was hitting a jag-time tune;
Back of the bar, in a solo game, sat Dangerous Dan McGrew,
And watching his luck was his light-o'-love, the lady that's known as Lou.

When out of the night, which was fifty below, and into the din and the glare,
There stumbled a miner fresh from the creeks, dog-dirty, and loaded for
bear.
He looked like a man with a foot in the grave and scarcely the strength of a
louse,
Yet he tilted a poke of dust on the bar, and he called for drinks for the
house.
There was none could place the stranger's face, though we searched
ourselves for a clue;
But we drank his health, and the last to drink was Dangerous Dan McGrew.

There's men that somehow just grip your eyes, and hold them hard like a
spell;
And such was he, and he looked to me like a man who had lived in hell;
With a face most hair, and the dreary stare of a dog whose day is done,
As he watered the green stuff in his glass, and the drops fell one by one.
Then I got to figgering who he was, and wondering what he'd do,
And I turned my head — and there watching him was the lady that's known
as Lou.

## The Poet

Wannabe cowboy, British-Canadian poet and novelist, Robert Service was variously called 'The Canadian Kipling' and 'The Bard of Yukon' [The Yukon is a territory in south west Canada]. Written during the age of the great gold rushes, Service's books of verses, as he modestly called them, and, later, his novels, became enormously popular, so much so that when Service lived in Paris in his middle years he was known as the richest author in the city. His first book of verses, *Songs of a Sourdough* [Yukon slang for old timer] earnt him in excess of $100,000, equivalent to about £2,000,000 today, unheard of riches for a poet. Though his writing was enormously popular, critical acclaim escaped him, with leading literary critics arguing Service's work was crude and derivative.

## The Poem

The title, of course, sets us up with expectations the poet can either fulfil or subvert. A familiar type of tale is quickly sketched out in long lines of ballad metre, called fourteeners, with seven beats and fourteen syllables. The metre propels this rough 'n' tough story along at a terrific lick, while the rhymes compulsively return us, like swivelling eyes in the saloon, to the principal players, McGrew, the stranger and Lou. Things are going to escalate quickly in this saloon, we guess.

McGrew's epithet tells us all we need to know about him. The 'dog-dirty' stranger, whose face can't be seen beneath a thick covering of hair, is the mystery man figure, familiar from cowboy films. He seems harmless enough, on the surface, of course, with 'scarcely the strength of a louse'. But, we know this sort of narrative, and clearly the stranger has some sort of bad-ass beef with Dangerous Dan and it's got something to do with the only female in the room, 'the lady's that's known as Lou'.

## The Teaching Ideas

➔     This is another poem that demands to be read aloud, ideally in a strong North American accent...

➜    What will happen next in this story? What's the stranger got against Dan? How does this mysterious man know 'the lady that's known as Lou'? Is that casual phrase, 'known as', significant perhaps? What will happen when McGrew sees the stranger looking at his beloved Lou? Trouble, we expect. How does Lou feel about Dan and about the stranger? How might this tale end? Pupils have two options: After discussing these questions and doing a little planning, they can either write the rest of the story in prose or, if they're feeling more poetically ambitious, they could have a go at maybe the next stanza in Service's swinging, rough 'n' ready ballad form.

After the first stanza, the stranger sits at the piano and plays a furious tune. Service gives us an insight into his feverish loneliness and his bitter thirst for revenge. Within a couple more stanzas we're on the cusp of violence:

The music almost died away ... then it burst like a pent-up flood;
And it seemed to say, "Repay, repay," and my eyes were blind with blood.
The thought came back of an ancient wrong, and it stung like a frozen lash,
And the lust awoke to kill, to kill ... then the music stopped with a crash,
And the stranger turned, and his eyes they burned in a most peculiar way;
In a buckskin shirt that was glazed with dirt he sat, and I saw him sway;
Then his lips went in in a kind of grin, and he spoke, and his voice was calm,
And "Boys," says he, "you don't know me, and none of you care a damn;
But I want to state, and my words are straight, and I'll bet my poke they're true,
That one of you is a hound of hell. . .and that one is Dan McGrew."

➜    Hopefully, their interest pricked, pupils will want to look up the rest of the poem and compare its ending with the one they planned and/ or wrote. Suffice it to say, this tale don't end up too good for none of them boys.

Although this ballad is infused with the trappings of the cowboy genre, the core story is a love triangle that could be played out in many different genres. Ask pupils to come up with various treatments of the story in the following genres: Gothic, soap opera, fantasy, dystopian/ Sci-Fi/ Jane Austen style romance... and any others you think might work.

# John Masefield [1878 - 1967]

## Cargoes

Quinquireme of Nineveh from distant Ophir
Rowing home to haven in sunny Palestine,
With a cargo of ivory,
And apes and peacocks,
Sandalwood, cedarwood, and sweet white wine.
Stately Spanish galleon coming from the Isthmus,
Dipping through the Tropics by the palm-green shores,
With a cargo of diamonds,
Emeralds, amethysts,
Topazes, and cinnamon, and gold moidores.
Dirty British coaster with a salt-caked smoke stack
Butting through the Channel in the mad March days,
With a cargo of Tyne coal,
Road-rail, pig-lead,
Firewood, iron-ware, and cheap tin trays.

## The Poet

Restless, sea-faring, sometime bee-keeping novelist, playwright and poet, John Masefield was the English poet laureate between 1930 and 1967. Trained by the merchant navy, Masefield travelled to the U.S.A. and Chile by sea, once deserting ship, aged just seventeen, and becoming, for a while, a vagrant, picking up what jobs he could to make ends meet.

## The Poem

This is another musical poem, all about the sounds and the dynamic rhythm. Afterall, what exactly is a quinquiereme[6] and where precisely is Nineveh? We don't really need to know and we can look the words up; picking up the sense that they are exotic things from exotic far-flung places is enough. The metre is highly unusual and could be scanned in a couple of ways. Take the first lines, for example.

The first could be scanned as regular anapestic tetramater:

Quinqui**reme** of Nineveh from **distant Ophir**
di - di - DUM di - di - DUM - di, di - DUM - di - di- DUM

Or, scanned as using our old, fancy-sounding friend the amphimacer:

**Quinquireme** of **Nineveh** from **distant Ophir**
DUM - di - DUM di- DUM - di - DUM, di - DUM - di - DUM

Whatever the interpretation of metre, what's certain is that it's already morphed by the second line:

**Row**ing **home** to **hav**en in **sunny Palestine**.

Notice too the thick weave of sounds that creates the rich sonic texture: Assonance in the first two words, alliteration between the second and fourth and the rhyme of 'sunny', 'paley'.

---

[6] Apparently, it was a type of Greek and later Roman Warship, similar to the Trireme depicted on the next page.

At other times Masefield combines mixed metrical feet in a way that shouldn't really work, but absolutely does. Take, for example:

**Sandalwood, cedarwood, and sweet white wine.**

Two amphimacers followed by the unstressed 'and' and then three emphatic stresses. Or, is that another anapestic line?

## The Teaching Ideas

➜     Teachers of a certain, distinguished vintage might just remember Jimmy McGovern's 1995 drama about teaching, **Hearts and Minds**. In this clip an idealistic rookie teacher, played by a frighteningly young-looking Christopher Eccleston, takes over a disenchanted old buffer's class on English poetry, with immediately electrifying effect. It'd be interesting to see what your pupils make of it. The poem the rooky teacher recites is, of course, *Cargoes*: https://www.youtube.com/watch?v=lhvCgzp8Zrs

➜   Pupils don't need to know the fancy technical terms for different metres. Sometimes, indeed, these can just get in the way of the poem. But trying to mark out the stresses could be fun and help highlight the room there is for literature and poetry, in particular, for different interpretations.

➜     Perhaps you could ask pupils to read the poem in pairs, one pupil reading, the other banging out the beat. They could try different versions by switching where the stresses might fall.

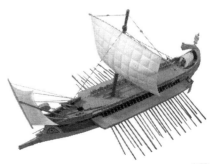

## Alfred Noyes [1880 - 1958]

### *The Highwayman*

PART ONE

The wind was a torrent of darkness among the gusty trees.
The moon was a ghostly galleon tossed upon cloudy seas.
The road was a ribbon of moonlight over the purple moor,
And the highwayman came riding—
    Riding—riding—
The highwayman came riding, up to the old inn-door.

He'd a French cocked-hat on his forehead, a bunch of lace at his chin,
A coat of the claret velvet, and breeches of brown doe-skin.
They fitted with never a wrinkle. His boots were up to the thigh.
And he rode with a jewelled twinkle,
    His pistol butts a-twinkle,
His rapier hilt a-twinkle, under the jewelled sky.

Over the cobbles he clattered and clashed in the dark inn-yard.
He tapped with his whip on the shutters, but all was locked and barred.

He whistled a tune to the window, and who should be waiting there
But the landlord's black-eyed daughter,
    Bess, the landlord's daughter,
Plaiting a dark red love-knot into her long black hair.

And dark in the dark old inn-yard a stable-wicket creaked
Where Tim the ostler listened. His face was white and peaked.
His eyes were hollows of madness, his hair like mouldy hay,
But he loved the landlord's daughter,
    The landlord's red-lipped daughter.
Dumb as a dog he listened, and he heard the robber say—

"One kiss, my bonny sweetheart, I'm after a prize to-night,
But I shall be back with the yellow gold before the morning light;
Yet, if they press me sharply, and harry me through the day,
Then look for me by moonlight,
    Watch for me by moonlight,
I'll come to thee by moonlight, though hell should bar the way."

He rose upright in the stirrups. He scarce could reach her hand,
But she loosened her hair in the casement. His face burnt like a brand
As the black cascade of perfume came tumbling over his breast;
And he kissed its waves in the moonlight,
    (O, sweet black waves in the moonlight!)
Then he tugged at his rein in the moonlight, and galloped away to the west.


PART TWO

He did not come in the dawning. He did not come at noon;
And out of the tawny sunset, before the rise of the moon,
When the road was a gypsy's ribbon, looping the purple moor,
A red-coat troop came marching—
    Marching—marching—
King George's men came marching, up to the old inn-door.

They said no word to the landlord. They drank his ale instead.

165

But they gagged his daughter, and bound her, to the foot of her narrow
bed.
Two of them knelt at her casement, with muskets at their side!
There was death at every window;
      And hell at one dark window;
For Bess could see, through her casement, the road that he would ride.

They had tied her up to attention, with many a sniggering jest.
They had bound a musket beside her, with the muzzle beneath her breast!
"Now, keep good watch!" and they kissed her. She heard the doomed man
say—
Look for me by moonlight;
      Watch for me by moonlight;
I'll come to thee by moonlight, though hell should bar the way!

She twisted her hands behind her; but all the knots held good!
She writhed her hands till her fingers were wet with sweat or blood!
They stretched and strained in the darkness, and the hours crawled by like
years
Till, now, on the stroke of midnight,
      Cold, on the stroke of midnight,
The tip of one finger touched it! The trigger at least was hers!

The tip of one finger touched it. She strove no more for the rest.
Up, she stood up to attention, with the muzzle beneath her breast.
She would not risk their hearing; she would not strive again;
For the road lay bare in the moonlight;
      Blank and bare in the moonlight;
And the blood of her veins, in the moonlight, throbbed to her love's refrain.

Tlot-tlot; tlot-tlot! Had they heard it? The horsehoofs ringing clear;
Tlot-tlot; tlot-tlot, in the distance? Were they deaf that they did not hear?
Down the ribbon of moonlight, over the brow of the hill,
The highwayman came riding—
      Riding—riding—
The red coats looked to their priming! She stood up, straight and still.

Tlot-tlot, in the frosty silence! Tlot-tlot, in the echoing night!
Nearer he came and nearer. Her face was like a light.
Her eyes grew wide for a moment; she drew one last deep breath,
Then her finger moved in the moonlight,
 Her musket shattered the moonlight,
Shattered her breast in the moonlight and warned him—with her death.

He turned. He spurred to the west; he did not know who stood
Bowed, with her head o'er the musket, drenched with her own blood!
Not till the dawn he heard it, and his face grew grey to hear
How Bess, the landlord's daughter,
 The landlord's black-eyed daughter,
Had watched for her love in the moonlight, and died in the darkness there.
Back, he spurred like a madman, shrieking a curse to the sky,
With the white road smoking behind him and his rapier brandished high.
Blood red were his spurs in the golden noon; wine-red was his velvet coat;
When they shot him down on the highway,
 Down like a dog on the highway,
And he lay in his blood on the highway, with a bunch of lace at his throat.

And still of a winter's night, they say, when the wind is in the trees,
When the moon is a ghostly galleon tossed upon cloudy seas,
When the road is a ribbon of moonlight over the purple moor,
A highwayman comes riding—
 Riding—riding—
A highwayman comes riding, up to the old inn-door.
Over the cobbles he clatters and clangs in the dark inn-yard.
He taps with his whip on the shutters, but all is locked and barred.
He whistles a tune to the window, and who should be waiting there
But the landlord's black-eyed daughter,
 Bess, the landlord's daughter,
Plaiting a dark red love-knot into her long black hair.

# The Poet

Playwright, short-story writer, poet and novelist, Alfred Noyes is remembered primarily for his ballad *The Highwayman*. Noyes must have been pretty confident in his abilities or, perhaps, just absent-minded, as he failed to get a degree because he'd arranged to meet a publisher when he should have been sitting a finals paper. Alongside his other work, Noyes wrote a science fiction novel, called **The Last Man**, in which almost the whole of humanity is wiped out by a death ray weapon.

# The Poem

It's terrifically exciting stuff isn't it, this tale of romantic love, dashing outlaws, dastardly soldiers, insane jealousy, cowardly betrayal, noble sacrifice and a love so strong it escapes the grave. True, it's not subtle, but this is a galloping ballad of dashing derring-do remember, and phrases that elsewhere would seem overwrought or clichéd, work well in this romping, broad-brush context: The wind is a 'torrent of darkness', the moon's a 'ghostly galleon' [granted, a rather hard image to visualise], the ostler's eyes are, of course, 'hollows of madness'.

The whole narrative is painted in rich, symbolic colours - reds and blacks and silvers, and is supplemented by aural imagery. The descriptions of the night, for instance, and of the highwayman are easy to visualise and we hear, through the poem's rhythm, the pounding of the highwayman's horse's hooves.

# The Teaching Ideas

➔   It's obviously a long poem, so pupils could be given sections to work on, contributing to a whole class reading. The aim would be to bring out the high-drama through a hammy OTT performance.

➔   The poem's heightened, almost cod-Romantic style make it very suitable for conversion into graphic novel or cartoon form. Rather than attempt to convert the whole narrative, pupils could select the parts they like the best. Another option would be to turn the poem into a film script, with suggested camera shots, dialogue, ambient sounds and so forth.

# William Carlos Williams [1883 - 1963]

## *This is Just to Say*

I have eaten
the plums
that were in
the icebox

and which
you were probably
saving
for breakfast

Forgive me
they were delicious
so sweet
and so cold

## The Poet

The Puerto-American modernist writer, William Carlos Williams was a practising doctor as well as a celebrated poet. Williams said he practised medicine during the day and wrote during the night. Though very different, the two halves of his work fed into each other, with the medical career granting the poet access, he said, to 'the secret gardens of the self'.

## The Poem

This stark, slight-looking, free verse poem illustrates the more minimalist side of W-C-W.'s poetry. Such writing always requires us to read between the lines. There are two ways to interpret the poem's tone; sincere or arch. If the apology is read as being sincere, the language of the poem betrays its speaker, inadvertently revealing how much he/ she enjoyed the stolen fruit, so 'delicious' and 'sweet' and 'cold', despite their apparent remorse. If the apology is read as slyly insincere, the lingering over the pleasure, those three adjectives, which are the only three in the poem, and the double intensifiers 'so sweet', 'so cold' are a kind of gleeful, comical rubbing it in. As youll see, my pastiche has punctuation; the original doesn't. Why might this be? Certainly, the lack of a full-stop at the end of W-C-W.'s suggests that this might not be the last word in this particular story...

## The Teaching Ideas

➔   W-C-W.'s poem is a great model for pupils. All they need to do is think of something they may have done which they really ought to feel bad about and maybe had to apologise for, but really in fact gave them pleasure. Obviously it can't be something too serious...The great thing about this exercise is that most pupils will be able to think of or make up an experience and write something very like a properly achieved poem.

Another possible creative writing: W-C-W. has written the poem in the form of a note for someone, perhaps his wife, to read and he didn't finish with a definitive full stop. How might his wife respond? *Thank you for telling me about the plums...I have some news too, about your car...* The pupils could write the wife's response to the apology, in verse, of course.

# This is Just to Say, Take #2

Accidentally
I smashed
That vase
Your parents

Bought us,
The one you always
told them
You really liked.

Forgive me.
But It made a
Tremendous crash
And it's cleared
A space.

For my trophies

# H. D., Hilda Doolittle [1886 - 1961]

## *Sea-Rose*

Rose, harsh rose,
marred and with stint of petals,
meagre flower, thin,
sparse of leaf,

more precious
than a wet rose
single on a stem —
you are caught in the drift.

Stunted, with small leaf,
you are flung on the sand,
you are lifted
in the crisp sand
that drives in the wind.

Can the spice-rose
drip such acrid fragrance
hardened in a leaf?

# The Poet

LGBT icon, Hilda Doolittle was an American poet and leading member of the Imagist movement. Even her poetic name, H. D., exemplifies the sort of compression of language demanded by the Imagists. The use of initials also, of course, makes the poet's name gender neutral.

# The Poem

Like W-C-W.'s, this poem is written in a stark and lean free verse style. In this case, the poem's thin, sculptural form is almost an example of concrete poetry. Unlike say *Jabberwocky* or *Cargoes*, sound in this poem is very secondary to this visual dimension.

Throughout the poem, H. D. forges a contrast between conventional ideas and depictions of beauty, as symbolised by a rose, with a different, harsher, less conventionally feminine aesthetic. This rose is not soft, fertile or voluptrous; H. D. celebrates a rose that is 'harsh', 'meagre', 'stunted' with few, 'small' petals. Rather than being cultivated and cared-for, it is 'flung' on the 'sand' and exposed to the 'drift' and the 'wind'. The final comparison is an image that could stand as a summary of the the poem itself, 'acrid fragrance / hardened in a leaf'.

# The Teaching Ideas

➜     The aesthetics of Imagism, the poetic movement of which H. D. was part, prioritised compression, clarity and intensity. The founder of the Imagist movement, Ezra Pound set out six tenets, concluding with the observation that, 'concentration is of the very essence of poetry'. H. D.'s distilled poem is spare, angular and fragile-looking on the page. Emphasise the concentrated qualities by presenting *Sea-Rose* first as prose and by adding some verbal padding. The pupils' tasks are to identify and cut away the padding and to re-arrange the prose as a poem. As before, five points for each rogue word they can spot. Help them out as much as you like, but it might be helpful to discuss, after a couple of readings, the gist of the poem and the aesthetic spareness characteristic of Imagist poetry.

'Rose, so harsh a rose, so marred and with such stint of petals, meagre, lean flower, thin, sparse of leaf, so much more precious than a wet rose single on a stem — you are caught, trapped, in the swirling drift. Stunted, with small leaf, you are flung haphazardly on the very wet sand, you are lifted up in the really crisp sand that drives so quickly in the cold as ice wind. Can the lovely spice-rose drip such acrid fragrance hardened in a green leaf?'

➜    Famously the Scottish poet, Robert Burns wrote 'O my love is like a red, red rose'. If you don't know this poem, how might the simile develop? Why have women often been compared to roses by men? How does H. D. continue, but also subvert the idea of women being like roses? If you give pupils the poem by H. D., i.e. without the explanatory Hilda Doolittle, ask them if they think it was written by a man or a woman, giving as many reasons as they can think of to support their attribution.

➜    What other conventional symbols of femininity and feminine beauty can pupils think of? A poet once compared a lovely woman to a summer's day, they might recall. What about symbols of masculinity? A very clever pupil might be about to mimic H. D.'s processes to write their own poem, critiquing contemporary ideas of beauty/ strength and femininity/ masculinity.

# Edna St. Vincent Millay [1892 - 1950]

## *Sonnet*

What lips my lips have kissed, and where, and why,
I have forgotten, and what arms have lain
Under my head till morning; but the rain
Is full of ghosts tonight, that tap and sigh
Upon the glass and listen for reply,
And in my heart there stirs a quiet pain
For unremembered lads that not again
Will turn to me at midnight with a cry.

Thus in the winter stands the lonely tree,
Nor knows what birds have vanished one by one,
Yet knows its boughs more silent than before:
I cannot say what loves have come and gone,
I only know that summer sang in me
A little while, that in me sings no more.

# The Poet

Beautiful, bobbed-haired, openly and brazenly bisexual, Pullitzer-Prize-winning American playwright and poet, Edna St. Vincent Millay must have cut quite a dash on the New York literary scene in the early decades of the twentieth century. A natural non-conformist, controversially frank, Millay was a feminist activist who wrote poems that expressed female experience in bold new ways. In accomplished sonnets she takes on, for instance, the traditionally male role of the playful lead in the game of love.

# The Poem

Milllay's beautiful, wistful and radical poem is a brilliantly achieved Petrarchan sonnet, the version of the sonnet form that is so demanding for writers in English. The poet has to fit the sense and the syntax to just five rhyme sounds, a tough task in comparison to the seven rhymes available in the Shakespearian version. Focus on the rhymes and you'll notice how the repetition in the octave suits the subject of repeated experience and how skilfully Millay tucks some of these rhymes away so that they don't stick out and wrench the poem's sinous flow. To achieve this, she uses a neat combination of caesuras and enjambment, ensuring both the eye and ear eased over and away from the echoing rhyme sounds.

# The Teaching Idea

➔    Present this sonnet to your class with one small amendment. Change the third word in the seventh line from 'lads' to 'girls'. Once the class have read the poem a few times ask them to together as much evidence as they can that the writer is male. Once you've discussed their ideas - which might include the frank admission to kissing and to a number of casual, casually forgotten lovers ['I cannot say what loves have come and gone'], the reference to the poet's lovers' cries and even the image of the poet as a phallic solitary tree, maybe also the fact that its a love poem and a sonnet at that - reveal the undoctored poem. Then pupils should be able to write a paragraph or two about how Millay challenges gender norms and, specifically, ideas of femininity and representation. Obviously, this work could build on your study of H. D. 's *Sea Rose* and presentations of masculinity elsewhere in this anthology.

# Anon.

## An Animal Alphabet

Alligator, beetle, porcupine, whale,
Bobolink, panther, dragon-fly, snail,
Crocodile, monkey, buffalo, hare,
Dromedary, leopard, mud-turtle, bear,
Elephant, badger, pelican, ox,
Flying-fish, reindeer, anaconda, fox,
Guinea-pig, dolphin, antelope, goose,
Humming-bird, weasel, pickerel, moose,
Ibex, rhinoceros, owl, kangaroo,
Jackal, opossum, toad, cockatoo,
Kingfisher, peacock, anteater, bat,
Lizard, ichneumon, honey-bee, rat,
Mocking-bird, camel, grasshopper, mouse,
Nightingale, spider, cuttle-fish, grouse,
Ocelot, pheasant, wolverine, auk,
Periwinkle, ermine, katydid, hawk,
Quail, hippopotamus, armadillo, moth,
Rattlesnake, lion, woodpecker, sloth,
Salamander, goldfinch, angleworm, dog,
Tiger, flamingo, scorpion, frog,
Unicorn, ostrich, nautilus, mole,
Viper, gorilla, basilisk, sole,
Whippoorwill, beaver, centipede, fawn,
Xantho, canary, polliwog, swan,
Yellowhammer, eagle, hyena, lark,
Zebra, chameleon, butterfly, shark.

# The Poet

A surprisingly prolific, protean poet, Anonymous has produced work in a wide of variety of styles, forms and idioms, covering a broad range of subjects. Written in male, female and neutral voices Anonymous' poems are always a little mysterious, prompting questions about the true character of their author. Their range is illustrated by how different this poem is from *Donal Og*.

# The Poem

As in says on the tin, this is an animal alphabet list poem. There may be a fiendishly complex, impossibly intricate code dictating the order of the animals that appear after the first one and before the last one in each line, but if so, it eludes me entirely. Although I did work out that, predominantly, the third animal is a trisyllable, which helps create a nice little hurrying up before the rhyme sound. The most important thing is that each animal in the middle of the lines contributes to the poem's relentless, bouncing tetrameter beat and the final one has to provide the couplet rhyme. The poet must have been relieved to come across or think of an 'auk'.

# The Teaching ideas

➔     This is another poem that should be fun to perform, best in small groups. If pupils are going to use choral voices, then getting the timing right will be essential; otherwise the words will become blurred by the multiple voices.

➔     Three final writing challenges: Challenge one, to write a line or a few more lines that could fit feasibly into the poem:

Mongoose, earwig, caterpillar, gnat
Narwhal, squirrel, polar bear, bat                     etc. Only better.

Challenge two is to write some lines for an alphabet poem in couplets of tetrameter, but about a different subject. Here are some possible topics: famous writers, food items, football teams, cars, girls' names, pop bands...

Challenge three, to complete the poem, going through the whole alphabet from A to Z.

**Activities: 14 things to do with poems**

1. Mash them (1) – mix together lines from two or more poems. The pupils' task is to untangle the tangled poems from each other.

2. Mash them (2) – the second time round make the task significantly harder. Rather than just mixing whole lines, mash the poems together more thoroughly, words, phrases, images and all, so that unmashing seems impossible. At first sight.

3. Dock the last stanza or few lines from a poem. Pupils have to come up with their own endings for the poem. Compare with the poet's version. Or present the poem without its title. Can pupils come up with a suitable one?

4. Break a poem into segments. Split the class into groups. Each group work in isolation on their segment and feedback on what they discover. Then their task is to fit the poem and their ideas about it together as a whole.

5. Give the class the first and last stanza of a poem. Their task is to provide the filling. They can choose to attempt the task at beginner level [in prose] or at world class level [in verse form].

6. Add superfluous words to a poem. Start off with obvious interventions, such as the interjection of blatantly alien, noticeable words. Try smuggling 'pineapple', 'bourbon' and 'haberdashers' into any of the poems and see if you can get it past the critical sensors.

7. Repeat the exercise – This time using much less extravagant words. Try to smuggle in a few intensifiers, such as 'really', 'very' and 'so'. Or extra adjectives.

8. Collapse the lineation in a poem and present it as continuous prose. The pupils' task is to put it back into verse. Discussing the various pros

and cons of various possible arrangements – short lines, long lines, irregular lines - can be very productive. Pay particular attention to line breaks and the words that end them. After a whatever-time-you-deem-fit, give the class the pattern of the first stanza. They then have to decide how to arrange the next stanza. Drip feed the rest of the poem to them.

9.   Find a way to present the shapes of each poem on the page without the words. The class should work through each poem, two minutes at a time, speculating on what the shape might tell us about the content of the poem. This exercise works especially well as a starter activity. We recommend you use two poems at a time, as the comparison helps pupils to recognise and appreciate different shapes.

10. Test the thesis that an astute reader can recognise poems by men from those written by women. Give the class one of the poems in this anthology without the name of the poet. Ask them to identify whether the writer is male or female and to explain their reasons for identifying them as such.

11. Split the class into groups. Each group should focus their analysis on a different feature of the poem. Start with the less obvious aspects: Group 1 should concentrate on enjambment and caesuras; group 2 on punctuation; group 3 on the metre and rhythm; group 4 on function words – conjunctions, articles, prepositions. 2-5 mins. only. Then swap focus, four times. Share findings.

12. In Observations on Poetry, Robert Graves wrote that 'rhymes properly used are the good servants whose presence at the dinner-table gives the guests a sense of opulent security; never awkward or over-clever, they hand the dishes silently and professionally. You can trust them not to interrupt the conversation or allow their personal disagreements to come to the notice of the guests; but some of them are getting very old for their work'. Explore the poets' use of rhyme in the light of Graves' comment. Are the rhymes ostentatiously original or old hat? Do they stick out of the poem or are they neatly tucked in? Are they dutiful servants of meaning or noisy disrupters of the peace?

13. The Romantic poet, John Keats, claimed that 'we hate poetry that has a palpable design upon us – and if we do not agree seems to put its hand its breeches pock'. Apply his comment to this selection of poems. Do any seem to have a 'palpable design' on the reader? If so, how does the poet want us to respond?

14. Each student pupil should crunch the poem being read down to one word per line. Discuss this process as a class. Project the poem so the whole class can see it and start the crunching process by indicating and then crossing-out the function words from each line. Now discuss which of the remaining words might be the most important. This will also give you an opportunity to refer to grammatical terms, such as nouns and verbs. Once each line has been reduced to one word, from this list, pupils should apply a harder crunch. This time all that should remain are the five most important words in the whole poem. Now they need to write two or three sentences for each of these words explaining exactly why they are so important and why the poet didn't choose any of the possible synonyms.

# Recommended Reading

Bowen et al. The Art of Poetry, vols.1-16. Peripeteia Press, 2015-17

Eagleton, T. How to Read a Poem. Wiley & Sons, 2006

Fry, S. The Ode Less Travelled. Arrow, 2007

Hayward, J. The Penguin Book English Verse, Penguin 1952

Heaney, S. & Hughes, T. The Rattle Bag. Faber & Faber, 1982

Herbert, W. & Hollis, M. Strong Words. Bloodaxe, 2000

Maxwell, G. On Poetry. Oberon Masters, 2012

Motion, A. Poetry by Heart. Viking, 2014

Padel, R. 52 Ways of Looking at a Poem. Vintage, 2004

Padel, R. The Poem and the Journey. Vintage, 2008

Schmidt, M. Lives of the Poets, Orion, 1998

Wolosky, S. The Art of Poetry: How to Read a Poem. OUP, 2008

Yates, C. Jumpstarts Poetry in the Secondary School. The Poetry Society, 1999.

# Great modern poems for KS3 pupils

Maya Angelou, *And Still I Rise*
John Agard, *Listen Mister Oxford Don*
W. H. Auden, *Refugee Blues; The Night Mail*
Simon Armitage, *Kid; Ten Pence Story* ; *; *The Shout; About his Person*
Liz Berry, *The Black Delph Bride; Nail-making*
John Betjeman, *Hunter Trials, Meditation on the A30*
Charles Causley, *What has Happened to Lulu; Timothy Winters*
Wendy Cope, *Two Cures for Love; Tich Miller, The Uncertainty of the Poet*
e.e. cummings, *anyone lived in a pretty how town*
Keith Douglas, *How to Kill*
Carol Ann Duffy, *Valentine, Medusa*
Vicki Feaver, *Judith*
James Fenton, *Out of the East*
Seamus Heaney, *Mid-Term Break*
John Hegley, *Jesus is not Just for Christmas*
Kathleen Jamie, *The Way we Live*
Tom Leonard, *Six O'clock News*
Liz Lockhead, *Men Talk*
Spike Milligan, *The Nin Nan Nong*
Adrian Mitchell, *Tell me Lies, Human Beings*
Roger McGough, *The Way Things Are; The Leader*
Ian McMillan, *Trainspotter*
Edwin Morgan, *The Loch Ness Monster's Song, Siesta of a Hungarian Snake*
Jack Ousby, *Gran can you rap?*
Wilfred Owen, *Dulce et Decorum Est*
Sylvia Plath, *Mad Girl's Love Song*
Jo Shapcott, *Tom and Jerry Visit England*
Owen Sheers, *Inheritance*
George Szirtes, *Song*
Dylan Thomas, *Do Not Go Gentle into that Good Night*
Benjamin Zephaniah, *Dis Poetry; Miss World*

## About the Author

Head of English and freelance writer, Neil Bowen has a Masters Degree in Literature & Education from Cambridge University and is a member of Ofqual's experts panel for English. He is the author of The Art of Writing English Essays for GCSE, co-author of The Art of Writing English Essays for A-level and Beyond and of The Art of Poetry, volumes 1-15. Neil runs the peripeteia project, bridging the gap between A-level and degree level English courses: www.peripeteia.webs.com.

From page 31, Spenser's sins and their matching modes of transport:

| | |
|---|---|
| Idleness | The ass |
| Avarice | The camel |
| Gluttony | The swine |
| Lechery | The goat |
| Wrath | The lion |
| Pride | She's the Queen, so has her own coach |
| Envy | The wolf |

Printed in Great Britain
by Amazon

62256024R00106